CONSTITUTIONAL TAX STRUCTURE

WHY MOST AMERICANS PAY TOO
MUCH FEDERAL INCOME TAX

CONSTITUTIONAL TAX STRUCTURE

BRIAN SWANSON

Copyright © 2018 by Brian Swanson.

Library of Congress Control Number:		2018912224
ISBN:	Hardcover	978-1-9845-5936-4
	Softcover	978-1-9845-5935-7
	eBook	978-1-9845-5951-7

All rights reserved. No part of this book may be reproduced or transmitted in any form or by any means, electronic or mechanical, including photocopying, recording, or by any information storage and retrieval system, without permission in writing from the copyright owner.

The views expressed in this work are solely those of the author and do not necessarily reflect the views of the publisher, and the publisher hereby disclaims any responsibility for them.

Any people depicted in stock imagery provided by Getty Images are models, and such images are being used for illustrative purposes only.
Certain stock imagery © Getty Images.

Print information available on the last page.

You may contact the author at: swansons6@hotmail.com

Rev. date: 11/14/2018

To order additional copies of this book, contact:
Xlibris
1-888-795-4274
www.Xlibris.com
Orders@Xlibris.com
786850

Though written constitutions may be violated in moments of passion or delusion, yet they furnish a text to which those who are watchful may again rally & recall the people: they fix too for the people principles for their political creed. — Thomas Jefferson

To John Adams, in hopes that you have not yet repented in heaven because there is a remnant in this country who loves liberty, the Constitution, and United States of America.

Disclaimer

The author of this book is not an attorney or a CPA. He does not offer legal advice, and this book is not intended to substitute for competent professional counsel should one be locked in a legal dispute with the United States Government. This book is intended to educate readers about the origin and extent of the Federal Government's taxing authority as defined in the United States Constitution.

The author and publisher of this book will accept no responsibility or liability for any loss or damage, financial, legal or otherwise, caused by or allegedly caused by, using the information in this book. The purchaser of this book must agree that any actions or decision when dealing with the IRS or other government agency are solely their own and that the purchaser will hold harmless both the author and publisher for any loss or damage of any kind when dealing with the IRS.

CONTENTS

I. Introduction 1
II. My First Challenge 4
III. How the Constitution Divides the Power of Taxation 15
    A. Direct and Indirect Taxes 15
    B. What is a "Direct Tax?" 17
    C. The Division of Financial Power 21
    D. The Federal Principle and the National Principle 27
IV. Principal vs. Income 33
    A. The Legal Distinction 33
    B. What Is Principal? 37
    C. What Is Income? 41
    D. Taxing Principal and Income 49
    E. What Is "Gross Income?" 54
V. The Purpose and Meaning of the Sixteenth Amendment 71
    A. Why Was It Adopted? 71
    B. What Did the Amendment Do? 76
VI. The Non-Apportioned Direct Tax Myth 81
    A. Origins 81
    B. Unlimited Tax 83
    C. Lower Courts in Revolt 87
VII. Why Americans Pay Too Much Federal Income Tax 90
    A. Legal Legerdemain and Terms of Art 90
    B. What Is Entered on Line 7 of a 1040? 94
    C. The Trap 99
    D. How to Respond to an Erroneous W2 102
VIII. Conclusion 106

I. Introduction

I began my serious study of the Constitutional Tax Structure and the Federal Income Tax in 2015 after reading Peter Hendrickson's book *Cracking the Code: The Fascinating Truth About Taxation in America*. Over the years, I would hear or read opinions of those who thought that there was something amiss in how our income tax laws were being applied, and while my interest was piqued here and there, I never did a serious investigation into it myself, and I never had any impulse to challenge the common understanding of the law. After reading Hendrickson's book, however, I found genuine insight that not only explained the tax with historical and legal clarity but also provided guidance on how to act on the information provided.

Reading his book was the beginning of my investigation into our tax system and income tax in particular, but it left me with a few unanswered questions. For example, I learned that "wages" as defined in the law is a legal term of art and that most Americans do not earn "wages" as defined, but I didn't know how to classify the money that I earned from my employment. If it is not "wages," then what is it? Also, the term "income" is described as this concept or idea that has no definite, legally fixed definition. I couldn't accept that. So, I kept researching. I needed to seriously investigate the Constitution and the tax laws for myself so I could explain them in detail, to my own satisfaction, in the event that I ever acted on my research. This investigation resulted in an even firmer and more resolute conviction that the current administration of the tax laws subjects the individual tax payer to financial injury and also threatens the foundation of our federal system of government.

I believe that I have discovered principles of American federalism that have been lost to history. Anyone with a rudimentary knowledge of the American system of government understands that the Constitution attempts to preserve liberty and promote effective government via division of authority and separation of powers. As many of our founders noted, people with political power cannot be trusted. So, while many readers will be familiar with the fact that political power is divided between the State and Federal governments, and then further divided between the three branches of government, the reader of this book will discover that financial power is similarly divided. The power of taxation and financial resources are divided between the State and Federal governments in the same way that political power is divided, and for the same reason: to protect the American people from tyranny and oppression. This is new. If not new, it is a rediscovery of an important element of federalism that had been lost to history.

This work is built on the works of those who have studied this topic before me. Many have written, posted, opined about the tax, and others have suffered for the actions they took based on their beliefs. The Federal Income Tax is a riddle wrapped in an enigma. It is intentionally difficult to understand, and its writers intended this to be so. It is a puzzle that has to be put together piece by piece, but the pieces are scattered among the Constitution, parts of the Internal Revenue Code, Supreme Court rulings, Congressional debates, and basic economics. Many of the pieces were found by others before this book was written. And while much of what has been written about the tax is nonsense, some careful investigators have been steadily gathering the correct pieces of the puzzle and putting them on display for the rest of us to consider, hoping that it might all be put together someday.

This book is not written for the novice. It's not technical or hard to understand, but those who have limited understanding of the Constitution and have never read a single section of the Internal Revenue Code may have difficulty following along. Not many words or pages are dedicated to explaining the law or basic constitutional concepts. An interest in American liberty and the principles on which it is founded is a prerequisite for reading this book.

This book represents the capstone on all that has been written before it. It brings all the pieces of the puzzle together and makes sense of them. When the reader finishes this book, the true nature of what is and is not "income," and why it must be what it is, will be understood, as well as how income fits into the overall Constitutional Tax Structure where financial resources are divided between the State and the Federal governments. Finally, the reader will understand the difference between capital and income, and will know the importance of differentiating between them in personal finance. (Capital is not reported on a Federal Income Tax form and nobody should be paying an income tax on their capital.)

II.   My First Challenge

Americans pay too much Federal Income Tax because they do not know the difference between capital and income. In 2015, I submitted my first Federal Income Tax return with the understanding that my earnings were not "wages" as defined. At this time in my research, I did not fully comprehend how to classify my earnings. I did not know that they were, in fact, capital. But I stumbled along the path to enlightenment with the limited truth I possessed, and kept searching. The result was a complete refund of all erroneously withheld money. Keep in mind that anything multiplied by zero is zero. So, if I earned no wages as defined, then all other elements of withholding based on wages are also zero: Social Security, FICA, Medicare, etc. All that erroneously withheld money was returned.

Since 2015, the Internal Revenue Service has ignored me. My 2016 and 2017 returns remain unprocessed to this day. The Service has neither challenged the calculations on my returns nor issued my refunds. Perhaps it hopes that I will go away. On my latest return, when I corrected my erroneous W2s using form 4852s, I asserted that the money paid to me is capital, and a direct tax on my capital requires apportionment. Declaring the correct legal character of the money in question, and identifying the correct constitutional rule that applies to it, is more powerful than declaring what it is not.

CONSTITUTIONAL TAX STRUCTURE

Saying it is "not wages" or "not income," while technically correct, is less assertive than saying "my money is capital" and challenging the Service to prove otherwise. In my opinion, this demonstrates a clearer understanding of the correct legal character of one's earnings.

<u>2015 Return Summary:</u>

- In 2015 I had no "income." I had no "gain derived from capital"; I had no financial gains from investment activity.
- In 2015, I had four sources of capital: earnings from McDuffie County, Georgia; earnings from Orange County, Florida; military retirement; and a teaching bonus from the Defense Accounting and Finance Service (DFAS).
    - o Capital from McDuffie County and Orange County was money paid for my own labor and represents minutes, hours, and days of my life. This money is my property and can only be taxed via apportionment. Total capital: $111,250.57.
    - o Capital from my military retirement and the teaching bonus was money I didn't earn from my own labor and qualifies as a privilege that may be taxed as an excise tax. Total capital: $29,044.76.
- I corrected the two W2s from McDuffie County and Orange County that reported to the IRS that the capital I earned qualified as "wages," using forms 4852. These two 4852s were sent to the IRS with my form 1040. The incorrect W2s were not sent.
- The two correct information returns (W2 and 1099R) from DFAS were also included with my 1040.

- The IRS, which is in possession of all these documents, sent me a letter asking me to explain my line 7 calculation.
- After my written explanation, my full refund was received including all withholding, Social Security, Medicare, and FICA (sum total of all withheld money on all forms). Well, almost all. Because of a ridiculous math error, I forgot to include the withholding on my 1099R military retirement. So my refund should have been $1,344.23 bigger.

CONSTITUTIONAL TAX STRUCTURE

2015 Information Returns:

Form W-2 Wage and Tax Statement 2015

Employer's Name, Address, and ZIP Code:
DEFENSE FINANCE & ACCOUNTING S
DFAS-CO-JJFKC
PO BOX 182317
COLUMBUS, OH 43218-2317

Employee's Name, Address, and ZIP Code:
BRIAN D SWANSON

State Wages, Tips, etc.: 1666.68
Local Wages, Tips, etc.: 1666.68

Department of Treasury - Internal Revenue Service

CORRECTED (if checked) — 12/14/2015

PAYER'S name, street address, city, state, and ZIP code:
Defense Finance and Accounting Service
US Military Retirement Pay
PO Box 7130
London, KY 40742-7130

PAYER'S Federal identification number: 34-0727612

RECIPIENT'S name, address, and ZIP code:
BRIAN DEAN SWANSON
...414-5975

1 Gross distribution: $27378.08
2a Taxable amount: $27378.08
2b Taxable amount not determined / Total Distribution
4 Federal Income tax withheld: $1344.23
7 Distribution code: 7
9 Your percentage of total distribution:
12 State income tax withheld: $0.00
13 State/Payer's state number:
$0.00

OMB No. 1545-0119 — 2015

Form 1099-R — Distribution From Pensions, Annuities, Retirement or Profit-Sharing Plans, IRAs, Insurance Contracts, etc.

Copy B — Report this income on your Federal tax return. This information is being furnished to the Internal Revenue Service.

RETIRED 01012015-12312015

W-2 (Orlando, FL)

1 Wages, tips, other comp.: 37518.80
2 Federal income tax withheld: 3845.30
3 Social security wages: 38638.74
4 Social security tax withheld: 2395.60
5 Medicare wages and tips: 38638.74
6 Medicare tax withheld: 560.26
d Control number: 0000001829 TH8 Dept. Corp. UQX6 1115
Employer's name, address, and ZIP code: ORLANDO, FL 32835
b Employer's FED ID number: 59-3721320
11 Nonqualified plans
14 Other: 1119.94
Employee's name, address and ZIP code: BRIAN SWANSON 34787
15 State Employer's state ID no.
2015

W-2 (Thomson, GA)

c Control Number: 443-0192
OMB NO. 1545-0008
This information is being furnished to the Internal Revenue Service.
1 Wages, tips, other compensation: 73731.43
2 Federal income tax withheld: 7031.57
3 Social security wages: 0.00
4 Social security tax withheld: 0.00
5 Medicare wages and tips: 78459.69
6 Medicare tax withheld: 1137.66
c Employer's name, address and ZIP code: THOMSON, GA 30824
7 Social security tips
8 Allocated tips
10 Dependent care benefits: 6.00
11 Nonqualified plans
12a See instructions for box 12: 0.00
12b: 0.00 12c: 0.00 12d: 0.00
b Employer identification number (EIN): 586000285
a Employee's social security number
13 Statutory employee / Retirement plan / Third-party sick pay / 14 Other
e Employee's name, address and ZIP code: BRIAN D SWANSON
15 State Employer's state ID No.: GA 5410064NW
16 State wages, tips, etc.: 73731.43
17 State income tax: 3436.82
18 Local wages, tips, etc.
19 Local Income tax
20 Locality name

Form W-2 Wage and Tax Statement — Copy B To Be Filed With Employee's FEDERAL Tax Return — 2015

Federal Filing Copy — W-2 Wage and Tax 2015

[stamped: "Fake News"]

7

BRIAN SWANSON

2015 Form 4852s used to correct erroneous W2s: Orange County:

Form 4852
(Rev. September 2014)
Department of the Treasury
Internal Revenue Service

Substitute for Form W-2, Wage and Tax Statement, or Form 1099-R, Distributions From Pensions, Annuities, Retirement or Profit-Sharing Plans, IRAs, Insurance Contracts, etc.
▶ Attach to Form 1040, 1040A, 1040-EZ, or 1040X.
▶ Information about Form 4852 is available at www.irs.gov/form4852.

OMB No. 1545-0074

1 Name(s) shown on return
Brian S~~~~~~

2 Your social security number
~~~~~~~~~

3 Address
2255 ~~~~~~~~~, Winter Garden, FL 34787

4 Enter year in space provided and check one box. For the tax year ending December 31, **2015**,
☒ I have been unable to obtain (or have received an incorrect) ☒ Form W-2 OR ☐ Form 1099-R.
☐ I have notified the IRS of this fact. The amounts shown on line 7 or line 8 are my best estimates for all wages or payments made to me and tax withheld by my employer or payer named on line 5.

5 Employer's or payer's name, address, and ZIP code
VIRTUAL SCHOOL
Orlando, FL 32835

6 Employer's or payer's identification number (if known)
59-3721320

7 Form W-2. Enter wages, tips, other compensation, and taxes withheld.
a	Wages, tips, and other compensation	0	f	State income tax withheld	0
b	Social security wages	0		(Name of state) . Florida	
c	Medicare wages and tips	0	g	Local income tax withheld	
d	Social security tips	0		(Name of locality)	
e	Federal income tax withheld	3845.30	h	Social security tax withheld	2395.60
			i	Medicare tax withheld	560.26

8 Form 1099-R. Enter distributions from pensions, annuities, retirement/profit-sharing plans, IRAs, insurance contracts, etc.
a	Gross distribution		f	Federal income tax withheld	
b	Taxable amount		g	State income tax withheld	
c	Taxable amount not determined ☐		h	Local income tax withheld	
d	Total distribution ☐		i	Employee contributions	
e	Capital gain (included in line 8b)		j	Distribution codes	

9 How did you determine the amounts on lines 7 and 8 above?
After a review of 26 USC and a careful self-assessment, I determined that the compensation I received for my labor was not "Wages" paid to an "Employee" as defined in 3121(a) and 3401(a), but the amounts withheld are correct.

10 Explain your efforts to obtain Form W-2, Form 1099-R, or Form W-2c, Corrected Wage and Tax Statement.
None.

General Instructions

Section references are to the Internal Revenue Code.

Future developments. The IRS has created a page on IRS.gov for information about Form 4852, at www.irs.gov/form4852. Information about any future developments affecting Form 4852 (such as legislation enacted after we release it) will be posted on that page.

Purpose of form. Form 4852 serves as a substitute for Forms W-2, W-2c, and 1099-R and is completed by you or your representatives when (a) your employer or payer does not issue you a Form W-2 or Form 1099-R or (b) an employer or payer has issued an incorrect Form W-2 or Form 1099-R. Attach this form to the back of your income tax return, before any supporting forms or schedules.

You should always attempt to get Form W-2, Form W-2c, or Form 1099-R from your employer or payer before contacting the IRS or filing Form 4852. If you do not receive the missing or corrected form from your employer or payer by February 14, you may call the IRS at 1-800-829-1040 for assistance. You must provide your name, address (including ZIP code), phone number, social security number, and dates of employment, and your employer or payer's name, address (including ZIP code), and phone number. The IRS will contact your employer or payer and request the missing form. The IRS will also send you a Form 4852. If you do not receive the missing form in sufficient time to file your income tax return timely, you may use the Form 4852 that the IRS sent you.

If you received an incorrect Form W-2 or Form 1099-R, you should always attempt to have your employer or payer issue a corrected form before filing Form 4852.

Note. Retain a copy of Form 4852 for your records. To help protect your social security benefits, keep a copy of Form 4852 until you begin receiving social security benefits, just in case there is a question about your work record and/or earnings in a particular year. After September 30 following the date shown on line 4, you may use a *my* Social Security online account to verify wages reported by your employers. Please visit www.ssa.gov/myaccount. Or, you may contact your local SSA office to verify wages reported by your employer.

Will I need to amend my return? If you receive a Form W-2, Form W-2c, or Form 1099-R after your return is filed with Form 4852, and the information differs from the information reported on your return, you must amend your return by filing Form 1040X, Amended U.S. Individual Income Tax Return.

Penalties. The IRS will challenge the claims of individuals who attempt to avoid or evade their federal tax liability by using Form 4852 in a manner other than as prescribed. Potential penalties for the improper use of Form 4852 include:

• Accuracy-related penalties equal to 20 percent of the amount of taxes that should have been paid,

• Civil fraud penalties equal to 75 percent of the amount of taxes that should have been paid, and

For Paperwork Reduction Act Notice, see page 2.   Cat. No. 42058U   Form **4852** (Rev. 9-2014)

CONSTITUTIONAL TAX STRUCTURE

McDuffie County:

Form 4852 (Rev. September 2014)
Department of the Treasury — Internal Revenue Service

Substitute for Form W-2, Wage and Tax Statement, or Form 1099-R, Distributions From Pensions, Annuities, Retirement or Profit-Sharing Plans, IRAs, Insurance Contracts, etc.

▶ Attach to Form 1040, 1040A, 1040-EZ, or 1040X.
▶ Information about Form 4852 is available at www.irs.gov/form4852.

OMB No. 1545-0074

1 Name(s) shown on return: Brian S█████

2 Your social security number: █████

3 Address: 2255 █████ Winter Garden, FL 34787

4 Enter year in space provided and check one box. For the tax year ending December 31, **2015**,
☐ I have been unable to obtain (or have received an incorrect) ☑ Form W-2 OR ☐ Form 1099-R.
☑ I have notified the IRS of this fact. The amounts shown on line 7 or line 8 are my best estimates for all wages or payments made to me and tax withheld by my employer or payer named on line 5.

5 Employer's or payer's name, address, and ZIP code: BD. OF ED █████ GA 30824

6 Employer's or payer's identification number (if known): 586█████

7 Form W-2. Enter wages, tips, other compensation, and taxes withheld.
- a Wages, tips, and other compensation 0
- b Social security wages 0
- c Medicare wages and tips 0
- d Social security tips 0
- e Federal income tax withheld 7029.57
- f State income tax withheld 3436.82
  (Name of state): Georgia
- g Local income tax withheld . . . .
  (Name of locality):
- h Social security tax withheld 0
- i Medicare tax withheld 1137.66

8 Form 1099-R. Enter distributions from pensions, annuities, retirement/profit-sharing plans, IRAs, insurance contracts, etc.
- a Gross distribution
- b Taxable amount
- c Taxable amount not determined ☐
- d Total distribution ☐
- e Capital gain (included in line 8b)
- f Federal income tax withheld
- g State income tax withheld
- h Local income tax withheld
- i Employee contributions
- j Distribution codes

9 How did you determine the amounts on lines 7 and 8 above?
After a review of 26 USC in general and a careful self-assessment, I determined that the compensation I received for my labor was not "Wages" paid to an "Employee" as defined in 3121(a) and 3401(a), but the amounts withheld were correct.

10 Explain your efforts to obtain Form W-2, Form 1099-R, or Form W-2c, Corrected Wage and Tax Statement.
None.

General Instructions

Section references are to the Internal Revenue Code.

Future developments. The IRS has created a page on IRS.gov for information about Form 4852, at www.irs.gov/form4852. Information about any future developments affecting Form 4852 (such as legislation enacted after we release it) will be posted on that page.

Purpose of form. Form 4852 serves as a substitute for Forms W-2, W-2c, and 1099-R and is completed by you or your representatives when (a) your employer or payer does not issue you a Form W-2 or Form 1099-R or (b) an employer or payer has issued an incorrect Form W-2 or Form 1099-R. Attach this form to the back of your income tax return, before any supporting forms or schedules.

You should always attempt to get Form W-2, Form W-2c, or Form 1099-R from your employer or payer before contacting the IRS or filing Form 4852. If you do not receive the missing or corrected form from your employer or payer by February 14, you may call the IRS at 1-800-829-1040 for assistance. You must provide your name, address (including ZIP code), phone number, social security number, and dates of employment, and your employer's or payer's name, address (including ZIP code), and phone number. The IRS will contact your employer or payer and request the missing form. The IRS also will send you a Form 4852. If you do not receive the missing form in sufficient time to file your income tax return timely, you may use the Form 4852 that the IRS sent you.

If you received an incorrect Form W-2 or Form 1099-R, you should always attempt to have your employer or payer issue a corrected form before filing Form 4852.

Note. Retain a copy of Form 4852 for your records. To help protect your social security benefits, keep a copy of Form 4852 until you begin receiving social security benefits, just in case there is a question about your work record and/or earnings in a particular year. After September 30 following the date shown on line 4, you may use a my Social Security online account to verify wages reported by your employers. Please visit www.ssa.gov/myaccount. Or, you may contact your local SSA office to verify wages reported by your employer.

Will I need to amend my return? If you receive a Form W-2, Form W-2c, or Form 1099-R after your return is filed with Form 4852, and the information differs from the information reported on your return, you must amend your return by filing Form 1040X, Amended U.S. Individual Income Tax Return.

Penalties. The IRS will challenge the claims of individuals who attempt to avoid or evade their federal tax liability by using Form 4852 in a manner other than as prescribed. Potential penalties for the improper use of Form 4852 include:

- Accuracy-related penalties equal to 20 percent of the amount of taxes that should have been paid,
- Civil fraud penalties equal to 75 percent of the amount of taxes that should have been paid, and

For Paperwork Reduction Act Notice, see page 2. Cat. No. 42058U Form **4852** (Rev. 9-2014)

BRIAN SWANSON

2015 Form 1040 requesting my $14,968 refund:

| Form **1040** | Department of the Treasury—Internal Revenue Service (99) U.S. Individual Income Tax Return | 2015 | OMB No. 1545-0074 | IRS Use Only—Do not write or staple in this space. |

For the year Jan. 1–Dec. 31, 2015, or other tax year beginning , 2015, ending , 20 | See separate instructions.

Your first name and initial: **Brian** | Last name: S——— | Your social security number: ———

If a joint return, spouse's first name and initial | Last name | Spouse's social security number: ———

Home address (number and street). If you have a P.O. box, see instructions. **2255** ——— | Apt. no. | ▲ Make sure the SSN(s) above and on line 6c are correct.

City, town or post office, state, and ZIP code. If you have a foreign address, also complete spaces below (see instructions). **Winter Garden, Fl 34787**

Presidential Election Campaign
Check here if you, or your spouse if filing jointly, want $3 to go to this fund. Checking a box below will not change your tax or refund. ☐ You ☐ Spouse

Foreign country name | Foreign province/state/county | Foreign postal code

Filing Status
Check only one box.
1. ☐ Single
2. ☐ Married filing jointly (even if only one had income)
3. ☒ Married filing separately. Enter spouse's SSN above and full name here. ▶ Michele Swanson
4. ☐ Head of household (with qualifying person). (See instructions.) If the qualifying person is a child but not your dependent, enter this child's name here. ▶
5. ☐ Qualifying widow(er) with dependent child

Exemptions
6a ☒ Yourself. If someone can claim you as a dependent, do not check box 6a . . . .
b ☒ Spouse . . . .

c Dependents: (1) First name Last name	(2) Dependent's social security number	(3) Dependent's relationship to you	(4) ✓ if child under age 17 qualifying for child tax credit (see instructions)
H———	———	Daughter	☒
H———	———	Daughter	☒
S———	———	Daughter	☒
			☐

Boxes checked on 6a and 6b: **2**
No. of children on 6c who:
• lived with you: **3**
• did not live with you due to divorce or separation (see instructions)
Dependents on 6c not entered above
Add numbers on lines above ▶ **5**

If more than four dependents, see instructions and check here ▶ ☐

d Total number of exemptions claimed . . . .

Income
Attach Form(s) W-2 here. Also attach Forms W-2G and 1099-R if tax was withheld.
If you did not get a W-2, see instructions.

7	Wages, salaries, tips, etc. Attach Form(s) W-2	7	1666	68
8a	Taxable interest. Attach Schedule B if required	8a		
b	Tax-exempt interest. Do not include on line 8a	8b		
9a	Ordinary dividends. Attach Schedule B if required	9a		
b	Qualified dividends	9b		
10	Taxable refunds, credits, or offsets of state and local income taxes	10		
11	Alimony received	11		
12	Business income or (loss). Attach Schedule C or C-EZ	12		
13	Capital gain or (loss). Attach Schedule D if required. If not required, check here ▶ ☐	13		
14	Other gains or (losses). Attach Form 4797	14		
15a	IRA distributions 15a	b Taxable amount	15b		
16a	Pensions and annuities 16a	b Taxable amount	16b	27,378	08
17	Rental real estate, royalties, partnerships, S corporations, trusts, etc. Attach Schedule E	17		
18	Farm income or (loss). Attach Schedule F	18		
19	Unemployment compensation	19		
20a	Social security benefits 20a	b Taxable amount	20b		
21	Other income. List type and amount	21		
22	Combine the amounts in the far right column for lines 7 through 21. This is your **total income** ▶	22	29,044	76

Adjusted Gross Income

23	Educator expenses	23		
24	Certain business expenses of reservists, performing artists, and fee-basis government officials. Attach Form 2106 or 2106-EZ	24		
25	Health savings account deduction. Attach Form 8889	25		
26	Moving expenses. Attach Form 3903	26		
27	Deductible part of self-employment tax. Attach Schedule SE	27		
28	Self-employed SEP, SIMPLE, and qualified plans	28		
29	Self-employed health insurance deduction	29		
30	Penalty on early withdrawal of savings	30		
31a	Alimony paid b Recipient's SSN ▶	31a		
32	IRA deduction	32		
33	Student loan interest deduction	33	1778	18
34	Tuition and fees. Attach Form 8917	34		
35	Domestic production activities deduction. Attach Form 8903	35		
36	Add lines 23 through 35	36	1,778	18
37	Subtract line 36 from line 22. This is your **adjusted gross income** ▶	37	27,266	58

10

CONSTITUTIONAL TAX STRUCTURE

Form 1040 (2015) — Page 2

Tax and Credits

- 38 Amount from line 37 (adjusted gross income) .... 38 | 27,266 | 58
- 39a Check: ☐ You were born before January 2, 1951, ☐ Blind. ☐ Spouse was born before January 2, 1951, ☐ Blind. Total boxes checked ▶ 39a
- b If your spouse itemizes on a separate return or you were a dual-status alien, check here ▶ 39b ☐

Standard Deduction for—
- People who check any box on line 39a or 39b or who can be claimed as a dependent, see instructions.
- All others:
  - Single or Married filing separately, $6,300
  - Married filing jointly or Qualifying widow(er), $12,600
  - Head of household, $9,250

- 40 Itemized deductions (from Schedule A) or your standard deduction (see left margin) .. 40 | 6,300 | 00
- 41 Subtract line 40 from line 38 .... 41 | 20,966 | 58
- 42 Exemptions. If line 38 is $154,950 or less, multiply $4,000 by the number on line 6d. Otherwise, see instructions ... 42 | 20,000 | 00
- 43 Taxable income. Subtract line 42 from line 41. If line 42 is more than line 41, enter -0- ... 43 | 966 | 58
- 44 Tax (see instructions). Check if any from: a ☐ Form(s) 8814 b ☐ Form 4972 c ☐ _____ 44 | 96 | 00
- 45 Alternative minimum tax (see instructions). Attach Form 6251 45
- 46 Excess advance premium tax credit repayment. Attach Form 8962 46
- 47 Add lines 44, 45, and 46 .... ▶ 47 | 96 | 00
- 48 Foreign tax credit. Attach Form 1116 if required 48
- 49 Credit for child and dependent care expenses. Attach Form 2441 .. 49
- 50 Education credits from Form 8863, line 19 50
- 51 Retirement savings contributions credit. Attach Form 8880 .. 51
- 52 Child tax credit. Attach Schedule 8812, if required .... 52 | 96 | 00
- 53 Residential energy credits. Attach Form 5695 53
- 54 Other credits from Form: a ☐ 3800 b ☐ 8801 c ☐ ___ 54
- 55 Add lines 48 through 54. These are your total credits .... 55 | 96 | 00
- 56 Subtract line 55 from line 47. If line 55 is more than line 47, enter -0- ...... ▶ 56 | 0 | 00

Other Taxes
- 57 Self-employment tax. Attach Schedule SE 57
- 58 Unreported social security and Medicare tax from Form: a ☐ 4137 b ☐ 8919 .. 58
- 59 Additional tax on IRAs, other qualified retirement plans, etc. Attach Form 5329 if required .. 59
- 60a Household employment taxes from Schedule H 60a
- b First-time homebuyer credit repayment. Attach Form 5405 if required 60b
- 61 Health care: individual responsibility (see instructions) Full-year coverage ☐ .. 61
- 62 Taxes from: a ☐ Form 8959 b ☐ Form 8960 c ☐ Instructions; enter code(s) ___ 62
- 63 Add lines 56 through 62. This is your total tax .... ▶ 63 | 0 | 00

Payments
- 64 Federal income tax withheld from Forms W-2 and 1099 .. 64 | 14,968 | 39
- 65 2015 estimated tax payments and amount applied from 2014 return .. 65

If you have a qualifying child, attach Schedule EIC.
- 66a Earned income credit (EIC) 66a
- b Nontaxable combat pay election | 66b |
- 67 Additional child tax credit. Attach Schedule 8812 67
- 68 American opportunity credit from Form 8863, line 8 .. 68
- 69 Net premium tax credit. Attach Form 8962 69
- 70 Amount paid with request for extension to file 70
- 71 Excess social security and tier 1 RRTA tax withheld 71
- 72 Credit for federal tax on fuels. Attach Form 4136 72
- 73 Credits from Form: a ☐ 2439 b ☐ Reserved c ☐ 8885 d ☐ __ 73
- 74 Add lines 64, 65, 66a, and 67 through 73. These are your total payments .... ▶ 74 | 14,968 | 39

Refund
- 75 If line 74 is more than line 63, subtract line 63 from line 74. This is the amount you overpaid .. 75 | 14,968 | 39
- 76a Amount of line 75 you want refunded to you. If Form 8888 is attached, check here ▶ ☐ .. 76a | 14,968 | 39

Direct deposit? See instructions.
- ▶ b Routing number ● ● ● ● ● ● ● ● ● ▶ c Type: ☑ Checking ☐ Savings
- ▶ d Account number ● ● ● ● ● ● ● ● ● ● ● ●
- 77 Amount of line 75 you want applied to your 2016 estimated tax ▶ | 77 |

Amount You Owe
- 78 Amount you owe. Subtract line 74 from line 63. For details on how to pay, see instructions ▶ 78
- 79 Estimated tax penalty (see instructions) 79

Third Party Designee
Do you want to allow another person to discuss this return with the IRS (see instructions)? ☐ Yes. Complete below. ☑ No
Designee's name ▶ Phone no. ▶ Personal identification number (PIN) ▶

Sign Here
Under penalties of perjury, I declare that I have examined this return and accompanying schedules and statements, and to the best of my knowledge and belief, they are true, correct, and complete. Declaration of preparer (other than taxpayer) is based on all information of which preparer has any knowledge.

Joint return? See instructions. Keep a copy for your records.

Your signature | Date | Your occupation: Teacher | Daytime phone number (831)601-0116
Spouse's signature. If a joint return, both must sign. | Date | Spouse's occupation | If the IRS sent you an Identity Protection PIN, enter it here (see inst.)

Paid Preparer Use Only
Print/Type preparer's name | Preparer's signature | Date | Check ☐ if self-employed | PTIN
Firm's name ▶ | Firm's EIN ▶
Firm's address ▶ | Phone no.

11

BRIAN SWANSON

IRS Correspondence asking me to verify my line 7 calculation:

IRS Department of the Treasury
Internal Revenue Service

AUSTIN TX 73301-0034

OMB Clearance No.: 1545-0074
In reply refer to: 0625799341
July 27, 2016   LTR 12C   0 R
                 201512 30
                          00002755
                 BODC: WI

BRIAN SWANSON
                34787

021540

Social security number:
     BATCH 15523,14   18221-191-14402-6

Dear Taxpayer:

We received your Dec. 31, 2015, Form 1040 federal individual income tax return, but we need more information to process the return accurately. Unless required otherwise, send us your reply within 20 days from the date of this letter.

Enclose only the information requested and any forms, schedules or other information required to support your entries and a copy of this letter. Don't send a copy of your return unless we ask you to do so. Don't respond with a Form 1040X, Amended U.S. Individual Income Tax Return. We'll issue any refund due to you in about 6 to 8 weeks from the time we receive your response. If we don't receive a response from you, we may have to increase the tax you owe or reduce your refund.

To obtain the forms, schedules, or publications to respond to this letter, visit www.irs.gov or call 1-800-TAX-FORM (1-800-829-3676).

Provide more information on how you calculated $1,666.68 on line 7, Form 1040.

If you have questions about this letter, call the appropriate telephone number listed below:

  - 1-800-829-0922 (Individual-Wage Earners)
  - 1-800-829-8374 (Individual-Self Employed/Business Owners)
  - 1-800-829-4059 (Telecommunication Device for the Deaf, TDD)
  - 1-267-941-1000 (Outside of the United States), not toll-free

If you prefer, you can write to us at the address shown at the beginning of this letter.

If you want to send the information by fax, our fax number is 855-204-5020. Due to the high volume, we can't acknowledge receipt of your fax. Your faxed signatures will become a permanent part of your filing. Don't send another copy by mail. Doing so could delay the processing of your return. Be sure to put your taxpayer identification number on each page faxed. Include a cover sheet with the following information:

CONSTITUTIONAL TAX STRUCTURE

My written response:

5 August 2016

Internal Revenue Service
Austin, Tx 73301

Dear Mr. Krebs,

I received your letter dated 27 July, 2016 ref: 0625799341 asking how I calculated line 7 on my 1040.

Line 7 was calculated from a W2 from the Defense Finance & Accounting Service for $1,666.68.

Two form 4852s were sent correcting erroneous reporting because I believe that this compensation does not fit the definition of "wages" paid to an "employee" as defined in 26 USC. These were submitted with my original 1040 and I have provided more copies with this response.

I mistakenly included the erroneous W2s along with the 4852s that corrected them. If an amended return is required to correct this error, I will send one immediately.

Please send future correspondence to my current mailing address:

~~███████████~~
~~███████████~~

I hope this answers all your questions.

Sincerely,

Brian S~~██████~~

BRIAN SWANSON

2015 Refund Check:

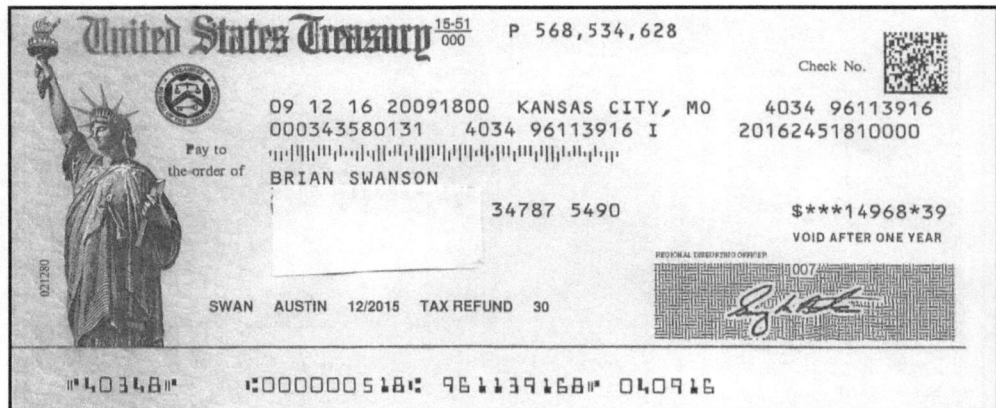

The IRS did not challenge my calculations and quietly issued my refund. I am a public school teacher and this job is my source of capital. The Federal Income Tax does not impose a direct tax on capital, and the IRS knows it. The IRS will return all erroneously withheld property to those Americans who know how to correctly differentiate between their capital and their "income" when calculating their "gross income" on their form 1040; the law requires it. I had no income in 2015. While I earned about $140,000 in capital during the year, only about $29,000 of it was subject to the tax. Hundreds of similar examples may be found on Mr. Hendrickson's website in the "bulletin board" section at losthorizons.com. Americans who report their capital as "wages" or as "income" are paying way too much Federal Income Tax.

The pages that follow remind readers of the difference between capital and income, explain why each is taxed differently in the Constitutional Tax Structure and reveal a forgotten truth that employment earnings are capital and not income.

III. How the Constitution Divides the Power of Taxation

The purpose of the Constitution of the United States is to provide effective government while preserving individual liberty. This is accomplished through division of authority and separation of powers. The Constitution delegates powers to the Federal Government and reserves for the States those powers not delegated. It also divides power between the executive, legislative, and judicial branches of government to provide checks and balances that promote stability. But seemingly lost to history is the idea that the Constitution divides the power of taxation between the Federal and State governments. The power of the purse is the principle power in politics, and preventing its concentration in one authority or another is essential to preserving liberty—so it follows that dividing the taxing power is consistent with the spirit and purpose of the Constitution. Additionally, the division of the taxing authority also serves to equitably allocate financial resources between Federal and State governments.

A. Direct and Indirect Taxes

The Constitutional tax structure will be constructed piece by piece like a puzzle and presented graphically to increase understanding. Like all our laws, the tax structure begins with the Constitution:

US Constitution

Article 1 Section 2:

> Representatives and direct taxes shall be apportioned among the several states which may be included within this union.

Section 8:

> Congress shall have Power to lay and collect Taxes, Duties, Imposts and Excises ... but all duties, imposts and excises shall be uniform throughout the United States.

Section 9:

> No capitation, or other direct, tax shall be laid, unless in proportion to the census or enumeration herein before directed to be taken.

The Constitutional tax structure as defined includes **direct taxes** subject to the rule of apportionment and **indirect taxes** (duties, imposts and excises) subject to the rule of uniformity. All taxes enacted by Congress are limited by either apportionment or uniformity, for there is no provision in our national government for an unlimited power of taxation. These limits protect citizens from misapplication and abuse and are explained by the Supreme Court in *Brushaber v. Union Pacific R. Co.* (240 U.S. 1, 1916):

> In the matter of taxation, the Constitution recognizes the two great classes of direct and indirect taxes, and

CONSTITUTIONAL TAX STRUCTURE

lays down two rules by which their imposition must be governed, namely, the rule of apportionment as to direct taxes, and the rule of uniformity as to duties, imposts, and excises.

The essential difference between direct and indirect taxes is summarized in *Knowlton v. Moore* (178 US 41, 1900):

> Direct taxes bear immediately upon persons, upon the possession and enjoyments of rights; indirect taxes are levied upon the happening of an event or an exchange.

Direct taxes are compulsory; one has no choice but to pay them. Indirect taxes are voluntary; one may avoid the tax by neither buying the item nor participating in the activity that is taxed.

These rules provide form to the tax structure:

US Constitution	
Direct Taxes	Indirect Taxes
Requirement: Apportionment	Requirement: Uniformity

B. What is a "Direct Tax?"

The Constitutional tax structure is dependent on the definition of the term "direct tax" since it appears in the Constitution. The Federal Government's taxing power is dependent on the legal definition of this term, and once "direct tax" is defined, the rest of the tax structure falls neatly into place. Justice Swayne noted in his opinion in *Springer v. United States* (1880) that:

> The question, what is a direct tax, is one exclusively in American jurisprudence. The text-writers of the country are in entire accord upon the subject.

"What is a direct tax" is a question exclusively encountered in American jurisprudence because this question is not a legal controversy in other countries. Foreign governments do not have constitutional limitations on their taxing authority; it is believed that the United States is the only government in the world that has restrictions on its sovereign power to tax.[1] Since the phrase "direct tax" appears in the Constitution, its definition is solely a judicial question, which means Congress has no power to define it. The Courts must provide a legally precise definition beyond the varying opinions of economists in order to ensure consistent application. David A. Wells, who helped President Lincoln create a system of internal revenue during the Civil War, observed that the Supreme Court:

> has felt compelled by the language of the Federal Constitution to assign to the term "*direct*," as applicable to taxation, a "*legal*" rather than *economic* definition.[2]

Since our government has need of a legal definition instead of an economic definition, the Supreme Court pronounced its legal definition in *Springer v. United States* (1880):

---

[1] David A. Wells, *Principles of Taxation*, Popular Science Monthly, July 1898 https://en.wikisource.org/wiki/Popular_Science_Monthly/Volume_53/July_1898/Principles_of_Taxation:_Theory_and_Practice_of_Income_Taxation_XXVIII

[2] Ibid, part 8, June 1897 https://en.wikisource.org/wiki/Popular_Science_Monthly/Volume_51/June_1897/Principles_of_Taxation:_Nomenclature_and_Forms_of_Taxation_XVII

CONSTITUTIONAL TAX STRUCTURE

> Our conclusions are, that direct taxes, within the meaning of the Constitution, are only capitation taxes, as expressed in that instrument, and taxes on real estate.

The Constitutional meaning of "direct taxes" is legally fixed by the Supreme Court. This decision created a logical construct where "direct taxes" and <u>*not direct*</u> taxes (indirect taxes) combine to embrace every conceivable power of taxation. This means that all taxes that are not "direct" are indirect. The meaning of "direct taxes" was slightly expanded by the decision in *Pollock v. Farmers' Loan and Trust* (1895), but that expanded meaning was later reversed by the Sixteenth Amendment. Chief Justice Roberts in *National Federation of Independent Business (NFIB) v. Sebelius* (567 U.S. 519, 2012) provides a complete summary of the constitutional meaning of "direct taxes":

> That narrow view of what a direct tax might be persisted for a century. In 1880, for example, we explained that "direct taxes, within the meaning of the Constitution, are only capitation taxes, as expressed in that instrument, and taxes on real estate." *Springer*, supra, at 602. In 1895, we expanded our interpretation to include taxes on personal property and income from personal property, in the course of striking down aspects of the federal income tax. *Pollock v. Farmers' Loan & Trust Co.*, 158 U.S. 601, 618 (1895). That result was overturned by the Sixteenth Amendment, although we continued to consider taxes on personal property to be direct taxes. See *Eisner v. Macomber*, 252 U.S. 189–219 (1920).

One will not find a more lucid or concise summary of the constitutional meaning of "direct taxes." First, they included only capitation taxes and taxes on real estate. *Pollock* expanded that interpretation to include "taxes on personal property and income from personal property," but that expanded interpretation was overturned by the Sixteenth Amendment. Note that the purpose of the Sixteenth Amendment is expressed in eight words, "that result was overturned by the Sixteenth Amendment": it overturned the Court's decision to expand the meaning of "direct taxes" to include income taxes. Therefore, while taxes on personal property are still included in the constitutional interpretation of "direct taxes," taxes on income are not included.

The Court's opinion on this topic is refreshingly consistent, as demonstrated by Chief Justice White's explanation of why a tax on income cannot be a "direct tax" in *Stanton v. Baltic Mining Co.* (240 U.S. 103, 1916):

> The Sixteenth Amendment conferred no new power of taxation, but simply prohibited the previous complete and plenary power of income taxation possessed by Congress from the beginning from being taken out of the category of indirect taxation to which it inherently belonged, and being placed in the category of direct taxation subject to apportionment by a consideration of the sources from which the income was derived.

Taxes on income cannot be direct taxes, because the Sixteenth Amendment prohibits the power of income taxation from being taken out of the category of indirect taxation, to which it inherently belongs: All taxation on income must remain in the category of indirect taxation, where the Federal Government can tax it without apportionment. After 102 years, it would seem that the Supreme Court's Constitutional interpretation of "direct taxes" and the meaning of the Sixteenth Amendment, as expressed by Chief Justice White through Chief Justice Roberts, remains perfectly consistent. "Direct taxes," within the meaning of the Constitution, are capitation taxes and taxes on real estate, which is interpreted to include taxes on all personal property, while all other taxes are indirect taxes.

The tax structure incorporating the meaning of "direct taxes:"

US Constitution	
Direct Taxes	Indirect Taxes
Requirement: Apportionment	Requirement: Uniformity
Capitation Taxes on Real Estate (Taxes on all personal property)	All *not Direct* Taxes including: Duties, Imposts and Excises (Taxes on Income)

C. The Division of Financial Power

Money is the only real power in this world. If the Constitution was written to divide power to protect against tyranny and oppression, then dividing financial power is just as important as dividing political power. Understanding this division of financial power may have been forever lost to history had it not been preserved in *Pollock v. Farmers' Loan & Trust Co.* (158 U.S. 601 & 618, 1895):

> In distributing the power of taxation, the Constitution retained to the State the absolute power of direct taxation, but granted to the Federal government the power of the same taxation upon condition that, in its exercise, such taxes should be apportioned among the several States according to number, and this was done in order to protect to the States, who were surrendering to the Federal government so many sources of income, the power of direct taxation, which was their principal remaining resource.

From this powerful revelation found in the syllabus, we can learn that the power of taxation is divided to fairly allocate financial resources and that apportionment exists to prevent the Federal Government from encroaching on the States' constitutionally protected source of revenue. Direct taxes are the States' principal financial resource, and all revenue derived from direct taxes belongs to the States unless apportioned for federal use. The States surrendered numerous sources of revenue to the Federal Government when ratifying the Constitution, so the absolute power of direct taxation is meant to compensate them and ensure they have a sufficient financial resource to fund their constitutional obligations. The following excerpt from Chief Justice Fuller's opinion in *Pollock* is quoted at length to provide authoritative evidence that, in the opinion of the Court, the Founders and the Constitution intentionally divided financial resources between the States and Federal Government, and that apportionment exists specifically to enforce the separation of financial power.

> The reasons for the clauses of the Constitution in respect of direct taxation are not far to seek. **The**

CONSTITUTIONAL TAX STRUCTURE

States, respectively, possessed plenary powers of taxation. They could tax the property of their citizens in such manner and to such extent as they saw fit; they had unrestricted powers to impose duties or imposts on imports from abroad, and excises on manufactures, consumable commodities, or otherwise. **They gave up the great sources of revenue derived from commerce**; they retained the concurrent power of levying excises, and duties if covering anything other than excises; but, in respect of them, the range of taxation was narrowed by the power granted over interstate commerce, and by the danger of being put at disadvantage in dealing with excises on manufactures. **They retained the power of direct taxation, and to that they looked as their chief resource**; but, even in respect of that, they granted the concurrent power, and if the tax were placed by both governments on the same subject, the claim of the United States had preference. **Therefore, they did not grant the power of direct taxation without regard to their own condition and resources as States;** but they granted the power of apportioned direct taxation, a power just as efficacious to serve the needs of the general government, **but securing to the States the opportunity to pay the amount apportioned, and to recoup from their own citizens** in the most feasible way, and in harmony with their systems of local self-government.

> The founders anticipated that the expenditures of the States, their counties, cities, and towns, would chiefly be met by direct taxation on accumulated property, while they expected that those of the Federal government would be, for the most part, met by indirect taxes. **And in order that the power of direct taxation by the general government should not be exercised, except on necessity…the qualified grant was made.**
>
> **(emphasis added)**

Then-US Attorney General Richard Olney, quoted in *Pollock,* provides a supporting opinion:

> [T]he power to directly tax realty and personalty was not meant for use as an ordinary, everyday power; that the United States was expected to rely for its customary revenues upon duties, imposts, and excises, and that it was meant it should impose direct taxes only in extraordinary emergencies and as a sort of *dernier resort.*

The Founders deliberately wrote into the Constitution a mechanism to divide and separate financial resources, and apportionment exists to enforce that separation. The Federal Government's primary source of revenue is from indirect taxes, while the States' primary source of revenue is from direct taxes. Apportionment restrains the Federal Government from imposing direct taxes except in times of emergency; otherwise, the Constitution leaves to the States all revenue derived from direct taxes. "To protect to the States the power of direct taxation" is the reason that the Federal Government must go

CONSTITUTIONAL TAX STRUCTURE

through the rule of apportionment to enact direct taxes. It's difficult by design. This difficulty acts as a barrier to protect the States' principal financial resource.

Therefore, the meaning of "direct taxes" is very important because it is the basis for understanding how the Constitution divides the power of taxation. Direct taxes are legally defined and are taxes on property; all other taxes are indirect taxes. The States' primary source of revenue comes from taxing a person's property, while the Federal government's primary source of revenue comes from taxing a person's activities.

The tax structure after dividing the power of taxation between the States and the Federal Government:

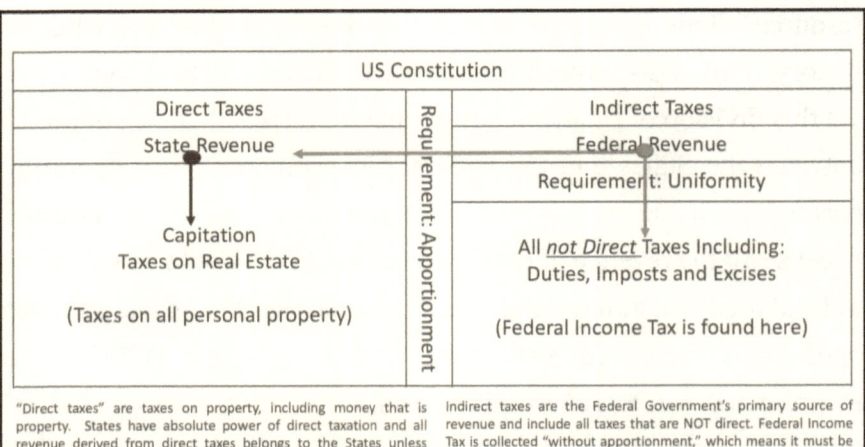

Those who understand the American government may admire how the Founders incorporated federalism into the tax structure and this chart is a visual representation of that structure. It depicts how apportionment divides financial resources between the Federal

Government and the States. When collecting federal revenue, Congress must follow the rule of uniformity to impose duties, imposts and excises (arrow down) or go through the rule of apportionment when it invades the States' protected source of revenue to impose "direct taxes" (arrow across). "Direct taxes" are the States' principle source of revenue, which the Constitution reserves exclusively for them, unless Congress reaches through the rule of apportionment to take some of that protected State revenue for itself. States may impose "direct taxes" without restriction, and the Constitution is silent on how they choose to impose indirect taxes within their own jurisdictions. Those agencies that peddle the myth that the Sixteenth Amendment authorizes a non-apportioned direct tax betray their ignorance of apportionment's function: "to protect to the States... the power of direct taxation, which was their principle remaining resource." This important element of federalism had been lost to history until rediscovered in *Pollock v. Farmers' Loan and Trust*, yet this division of financial power ensures a fiscal balance of power between the States and the Federal Government. When operating correctly, it's likely that the States would never need federal aid because all the revenue derived from direct taxes would be sufficient to fund their constitutional duties. However, the system has not been operating correctly for some time. Perhaps as much as $2 trillion in protected State Government revenue is going into the federal treasury, when that money should never leave the States.

The importance of rediscovering this lost element of federalism cannot be exaggerated. This knowledge, when given its proper consideration, may prove that many lower court rulings regarding the income tax and the Sixteenth Amendment are flawed. The purpose of apportionment is to protect to the States the power of direct taxation, but a non-apportioned direct tax would defeat that purpose by permitting the Federal Government to raid the States' constitutionally protected source of revenue with impunity. This would destroy the State Governments' financial and political independence, undermine their sovereignty, and threaten the foundation of our federal system of government.

D. The Federal Principle and the National Principle

In "Federalist 39," James Madison concluded that our Constitution created a government that is neither wholly national nor wholly federal, but a combination of both, explaining the difference this way:

> The difference between a federal and national government, as it relates to the operation of the government, is supposed to consist in this, that in the former the powers operate on the political bodies composing the Confederacy, in their political capacities; in the latter, on the individual citizens composing the nation, in their individual capacities.

The federal and national principles of government are manifest in the tax structure. The rule of uniformity has the effect of stripping away the State boundaries to collect indirect taxes on citizens composing the nation, in their individual capacities, as if the country is one consolidated republic. In contrast, direct taxes are apportioned and collected from each of the States in their political capacities. The rule of uniformity promotes the national principle while the rule of apportionment promotes the federal principle, so it could be said that indirect taxes are collected *nationally* while direct taxes are collected *federally,* and in harmony with Madison's conclusion, the Constitutional Tax Structure is partly national and partly federal.

This means that individual citizens pay indirect taxes, while the State Governments pay direct taxes. Justice Paterson, in *Hylton v. United States* (3 U.S. 3 Dall. 171 171, 1796), observed:

> **Apportionment is an operation on states**, and involves valuations and assessments which are arbitrary, and should not be resorted to but in case of necessity. **Uniformity is an instant operation on individuals** without the intervention of assessments or any regard to states, and is at once easy, certain, and efficacious

- Direct taxes are **apportioned** and operate on **States**.
- Indirect taxes are **uniform** and operate on **individuals.**

These rules determine the operation of the tax: uniform taxes operate on individuals and apportioned taxes operate on States. The Constitution does not permit these rules to be altered or rearranged for the sake of convenience. The Constitution does not authorize a uniform direct tax or an apportioned indirect tax, and neither Congress nor the IRS can invent a new tax. Therefore, direct taxes do not operate on individuals and indirect taxes do not operate on States, because there is no provision for direct taxes to be uniform or indirect taxes to be apportioned as shown in the graphic below:

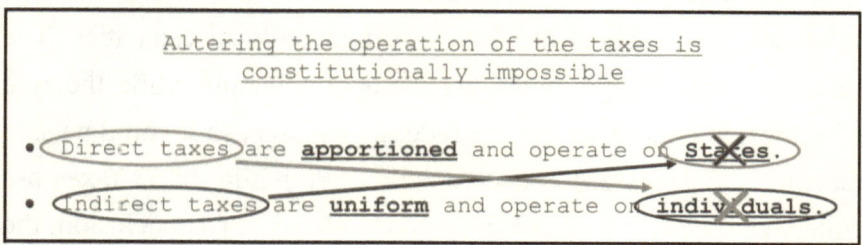

CONSTITUTIONAL TAX STRUCTURE

Chief Justice Roberts provided contemporary analysis to support the premise that the States pay direct taxes in *NFIB,* where he explains Article 1 Section 9:

> That clause provides: "No Capitation, or other direct, Tax shall be laid, unless in Proportion to the Census or Enumeration herein before directed to be taken." This requirement means that any "direct Tax" must be apportioned so that each State pays in proportion to its population.[3]

Roberts explains that when Congress imposes a direct tax, "each State pays in proportion to its population," from which it can be concluded that the individual does not pay a direct tax. When Congress enacts a direct tax, the State Governments write the checks to pay it. Chief Justice Fuller's explanation in *Pollock* is in accord with Roberts's opinion, as Fuller expects the States "to pay the amount apportioned and to recoup from their own citizens"[4] the amount of the federal tax. An example of a direct tax imposed by Congress in 1813 can be found in the *Statues at Large*, Vol. 3, Page 53, Chapter 37 and is shown here:

---

[3] *NFIB,* supra.

[4] *Pollock,* supra.

> CHAP. XXXVII.—*An Act to lay and collect a direct tax within the United States.* (b)   August 2, 1813.
>
> *Be it enacted by the Senate and House of Representatives of the United States of America in Congress assembled,* That a direct tax of three millions of dollars shall be and is hereby laid upon the United States, and apportioned to the states respectively, in the manner following:
>
> Act of July 22, 1813, ch. 13.
>
> Apportionment.
>
> To the state of New Hampshire, ninety-six thousand seven hundred ninety-three dollars and thirty-seven cents. — New Hampshire.
>
> To the state of Massachusetts, three hundred sixteen thousand two hundred seventy dollars and ninety-eight cents. — Massachusetts.
>
> To the state of Rhode Island, thirty-four thousand seven hundred two dollars and eighteen cents. — Rhode Island.
>
> To the state of Connecticut, one hundred eighteen thousand one hundred sixty-seven dollars and seventy-one cents. — Connecticut.
>
> To the state of Vermont, ninety-eight thousand three hundred forty-three dollars and seventy-one cents. — Vermont.
>
> To the state of New York, four hundred thirty thousand one hundred forty-one dollars and sixty-two cents. — New York.
>
> To the state of New Jersey, one hundred eight thousand eight hundred seventy-one dollars and eighty-three cents. — New Jersey.
>
> To the state of Pennsylvania, three hundred sixty-five thousand four hundred seventy-nine dollars and sixteen cents. — Pennsylvania.
>
> To the state of Delaware, thirty-two thousand forty-six dollars and twenty-five cents. — Delaware.
>
> To the state of Maryland, one hundred fifty-one thousand six hundred twenty-three dollars and ninety-four cents. — Maryland.
>
> To the state of Virginia, three hundred sixty-nine thousand eighteen dollars and forty-four cents. — Virginia.
>
> To the state of Kentucky, one hundred sixty-eight thousand nine hundred twenty-eight dollars and seventy-six cents. — Kentucky.
>
> To the state of Ohio, one hundred four thousand one hundred fifty dollars and fourteen cents. — Ohio.
>
> To the state of North Carolina, two hundred twenty thousand two hundred thirty-eight dollars and twenty-eight cents. — North Carolina.
>
> To the state of Tennessee, one hundred ten thousand eighty-six dollars and fifty-five cents. — Tennessee.
>
> ---
> (a) Notes of the naturalization acts, vol. i. 103.
> (b) See notes of acts relating to the assessment of lands for the direct taxes, and the acts for the collection of direct taxes, vol. i. 580.

As can be seen, the State pays a direct tax. Therefore, not only is the power of taxation divided between the States and the Federal Government, but who pays the tax is also divided. Direct taxes are collected federally and are paid by the States, not by individuals.

The Internal Revenue Service has a different opinion, as shown on its website where it describes the Federal Income Tax as a non-apportioned direct tax:

> Some individuals and groups assert that the Sixteenth Amendment does not authorize a direct non-apportioned income tax and, thus, U.S. citizens and residents are not subject to federal income tax laws.

CONSTITUTIONAL TAX STRUCTURE

The Law: The constitutionality of the Sixteenth Amendment has invariably been upheld when challenged. Numerous courts have both implicitly and explicitly recognized that the Sixteenth Amendment authorizes a non-apportioned direct income tax on United States citizens and that the federal tax laws are valid as applied.[5]

The IRS believes that United States citizens pay direct taxes. However, *Hylton* tells us that "uniformity is an instant operation on individuals," and *Knowlton v. Moore* (178 US 41, 1900) tells us that uniformity is imposed "**only** on duties, imposts and excises"—not direct taxes:

> Thus, the qualification of uniformity is imposed not upon all taxes which the Constitution authorizes, but only on duties, imposts and excises.

Therefore, only duties, imposts and excises operate on individuals. The rule of uniformity does not apply to direct taxes, and consequently direct taxes cannot operate on individuals. *Brushaber v. Union Pacific R. Co.* (240 U.S. 1) provides a supporting opinion:

> Second, that the contention that the Amendment treats a tax on income as a direct tax although it is relieved from apportionment **and is necessarily therefore not subject to the rule of uniformity, as such rule only applies to taxes which are not direct.**
>
> **(emphasis added)**

---

[5] IRS webpage: https://www.irs.gov/tax-professionals/the-truth-about-frivolous-tax-arguments-section-i-d-to-e#_Toc350157906

Uniformity operates on individuals and "**only applies** to taxes which are **not direct**." So there is no such tax as a uniform direct tax, and trying to disguise it by calling it a "non-apportioned direct tax" is fruitless because there is no direct tax that operates on individuals, regardless how it is described. Unfortunately for the IRS, United States citizens cannot pay direct taxes; State Governments pay direct taxes while individuals pay indirect taxes. Such is the effect of federalism incorporated into the tax structure.

IV. Principal vs. Income

A. The Legal Distinction

<u>Because of our dual system of government, all money is separated into two Constitutional categories:</u>

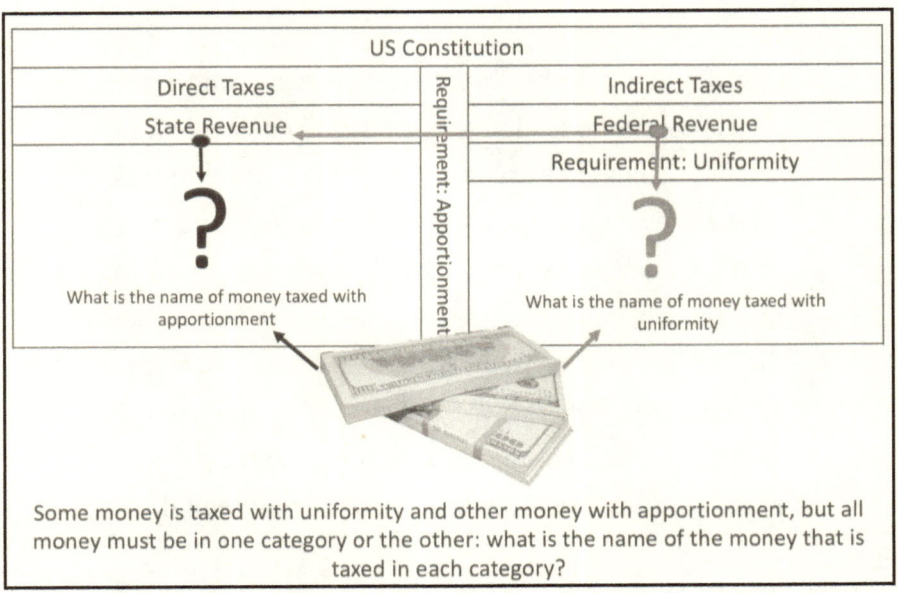

The United States has a dual system of government. Power is divided between the State and Federal governments and this creates a dual legal structure with separate jurisdictions. This dual system is manifest in the tax structure and creates a requirement for two constitutional categories for money. If money is in one constitutional category, the Congress can tax it without apportionment. However, if money is in the other constitutional category, the Congress can't touch it unless it is apportioned because a tax on that money is a source of revenue the Constitution reserves to the States. All money must be in one of these two categories.

The senators who debated the first Federal Income Tax, after the ratification of the Sixteenth Amendment in 1913, understood these two categories of money and their legal significance. Reviewing the debates from the 1913 Congressional Record, modern Americans may learn many economic lessons. Senator Cummins from Iowa took the floor and gave us a lesson on the two constitutional categories of money:

> ...It ought not to be forgotten, however—and I am now speaking to the lawyers on the other side; I want to make a lawyer's argument and not to raise at this moment any question of policy—that the authority of the Congress of the United States with regard to this subject is not unlimited. Our power is not like the power which Great Britain exercises over the subject. It is not like the power which the several States exercise over the subject. It is a power granted in article 16 of the Constitution, and I will read it:
>
> *Congress shall have power to lay and collect taxes on incomes, from whatever source derived, without*

CONSTITUTIONAL TAX STRUCTURE

apportionment among the several States, and without regard to any census or enumeration.

Our authority is to levy a tax upon incomes. I take it that every lawyer will agree with me in the conclusion that we cannot levy under this amendment a tax upon anything but an income. I assume that every lawyer will agree with me that we cannot legislatively interpret the meaning of the word "income." That is purely a judicial matter. We cannot enlarge the meaning of the Word "income." We need not levy our tax upon the entire income. We may levy it upon part of an income, but we cannot levy it upon anything but an income; and what is an income must be determined by the courts of the country when the question is submitted to them.[6]

Senator Fletcher from Florida interrupted to ask an incisive question:

I should like to inquire whether the Senator means to state that Congress cannot by statute define what shall be regarded as an income tax?[7]

Senator Cummins' response is enlightening and instructive:

I do not think so, Mr. President. The word "income" had a well-defined meaning before the amendment of the Constitution was adopted. It has been defined in all the courts of this country. When the people of

---

[6] Congressional Record, Vol. L Part IV, pg. 3843
[7] Ibid.

the country granted to Congress the right to levy a tax on incomes, that right was granted with reference to the legal meaning and interpretation of the word "income" as it was then or as it might thereafter be defined or understood in legal procedure. **If we could call anything income that we pleased, we could obliterate all the distinction between income and principal.** Whenever this law comes to be tested in the courts of the country, it will be found that the courts will undertake to declare whether the thing upon which we levy the tax is income or whether it is something else.[8]

(emphasis added)

Later in the debate, Senator Cummins made this statement:

The people have granted us the power to levy a tax on incomes, and it will always be a judicial question as to whether a particular thing is **income or whether it is principal**.[9]

(emphasis added)

Income and principal are the two constitutional categories of money. All money, no matter what other terms may be used to describe it (like wages, salaries, tips, or commissions), must fall into one of these two categories. The Supreme Court confirmed these two categories of money in *Doyle v. Mitchell Bros Co.* (247 U.S. 179, 1918):

---

[8] Ibid

[9] Ibid, pg. 3844

CONSTITUTIONAL TAX STRUCTURE

> Whatever difficulty there may be about a precise and scientific definition of "income," it imports, as used here, **something entirely distinct from principal or capital** either as a subject of taxation or as a measure of the tax.
>
> **(emphasis added)**

Income and principal (or capital) are the two categories of money and they are defined according to legal procedure; this legal distinction must be strictly enforced because of our dual system of government.

B. What Is Principal?

Knowing that principal (or capital) is one category of money doesn't explain what it is in the legal or constitutional sense. The senators who gave us that first income tax in 1913 understood it, and thankfully their debates are recorded so we can learn from them. Senator Sherman made the following observation:

> If by professional effort any person should earn a given sum annually and he spends half of it, he saves the other half. The half so saved in turn becomes **principal**. That principal is **property**.[10]
>
> **(emphasis added)**

Principal is the money one saves after a year's labor, and this principal is property. Senator Williams added:

---

[10] Congressional Record, Vol. L Part IV pg. 3843

> **Money** is as much property as is anything else, and when a man earns $20,000 in money during a year he has got that much in **property**.[11]
>
> **(emphasis added)**

The money a person earns is their property and it must be taxed as property. This means it must be apportioned, and apportioned taxes are rarely enacted. Senator Williams observed:

> so that the man whose **property** consists in dollars which he earns in a year is the least taxed of all men.[12]
>
> **(emphasis added)**

The Sixteenth Amendment allows a tax on income without apportionment, not a tax on all money that a person earns. The money that is income is separate from the money that is property. Senator Cummins added:

> If it were within the power of Congress to enlarge the meaning of the word "income," it could, as I suggested a moment ago, obliterate all difference between income and principal, **and obviously the people of this country did not intend to give to Congress the power to levy a direct tax upon all the property of this country without apportionment.**[13]
>
> **(emphasis added)**

---

[11] Ibid, pg. 3838

[12] Ibid, pg. 3839

[13] Ibid, pg. 3844

CONSTITUTIONAL TAX STRUCTURE

Only *income* can be taxed without apportionment, not money that is principal or property. "Property" is not a reference to a house or car, it means the money earned from one's own effort. The money earned from individual labor is personal property because labor is personal property, as the Supreme Court unequivocally confirmed in *Butchers' Union v. Crescent City Co.* (111 U.S. 746, 1884):

> The property which every man has in his own labor,
> as it is the original foundation of all other property,
> so it is the most sacred and inviolable.

The property people have in their own labor is the most sacred and inviolable because it represents a part of their life. When one surrenders a part of their life in exchange for money, that money represents minutes, hours, and days of their life that cannot be recovered and this is what makes money property. That portion of one's life that is converted into money remains their personal property, as described by *Doyle v. Mitchell Bros Co.* (247 U.S. 179, 1918):

> When the act took effect, plaintiff's timber lands,
> with whatever value they then possessed, were a part
> of its capital assets, and a subsequent change of form
> by conversion into money did not change the essence.

The change in form does not change the essence: an asset class does not change legal status when it is converted into money. In the same way that the conversion of timber into money remained a capital asset, so the conversion of labor into money remains personal property. The conversion of property from labor into money is the conversion of a capital asset from one form into another; this describes how individual labor creates financial capital.

Life and labor are capital assets. Financial capital (or principal) originates from individual labor, which is the source of all property. Abraham Lincoln, in his first Annual Message, supported this conclusion:

> Labor is prior to and independent of capital. Capital is only the fruit of labor, and could never have existed if labor had not first existed.

Capital is created by individual labor:

1. A business makes an $800 capital investment into labor; this $800 transfer of capital is his paycheck. His newly acquired capital can be spent, saved or invested.
2. The worker adds $1000 in value to the business.
3. The business recovers its $800 capital investment and has $200 profit. This profit is the business' increased capital. Business operations produce profits and these profits represent increased capital, which can be spent, saved or invested.

The worker has created $1000 in capital. As a result of his work, he has converted his labor into $800 in financial capital for himself and $200 profit for the business.

Financial capital is the fruit of one's own labor and usually comes in the form of a paycheck. At the end of a week, 40 hours of life's capital has been exhausted and in exchange, one receives 40 hours' worth of financial capital. The paycheck restores capital so at the end of the week, one has the same amount of capital as at the beginning. The capital is merely in a different form and the "change of form

CONSTITUTIONAL TAX STRUCTURE

by conversion into money did not change the essence": when life and labor are converted into money, the money remains capital. Compensation for labor is capital regardless of whether it is paid by the Federal Government, a private employer, or your neighbor down the street. If the capital is acquired by a privilege, it will affect how the capital gets taxed as described later. But once acquired, capital can be spent, capital can be saved, or capital can be invested.

The principle is the same for a business. Business operations create profits and these profits represent increased capital. If the business begins the day with $100 in the cash register, this cash is capital. At the end of a successful business day, if the business has $1,000 in the register, it has $900 profit and $900 in increased capital. A business with $10 million in profit has created $10 million in **capital**.

If what is written here is not true—if business and employment activities do not create capital—then the question must be asked: where does capital originate in our capitalist economy? The ability to distinguish between money that is property and money that is income is an important piece of the income tax puzzle.

Principal is capital—it is property and it originates with any trade, profession, job, or occupation whatsoever. Principal is the product of individual labor and is one constitutional category of money.

C. What Is Income?

The Sixteenth Amendment authorizes Congress to levy a tax on incomes without apportionment. The Amendment does not authorize a tax upon anything but an income. The object of the tax must be an income to fall within the authority of the Amendment and must be legally distinct from principal or capital. Since "income" appears in the Constitution, Congress cannot by legislation alter the meaning of "income,"[14] and it will always be a judicial question whether a tax falls on income or principal. The Supreme Court confirmed this analysis in *Eisner v. Macomber* (252 U.S. 189, 1920):

> it becomes essential to distinguish between what is and what is not "income," as the term is there used, and to apply the distinction, as cases arise, according to truth and substance, without regard to form. Congress cannot by any definition it may adopt conclude the matter, since it cannot by legislation alter the Constitution.

The courts must establish the legal relationship between the two categories of money to distinguish between that money which is property and that money which is income. The legal relationship is decided according to truth and substance, not semantics or rhetorical trickery. The Constitution prohibits Congress from defining as "income" money that is property because a tax on property must be apportioned but an apportioned "income" tax is prohibited; the two must remain legally distinct from each other. The senators who debated the 1913 income tax thought this, too. The court's duty to distinguish between these categories of money is clearly explained by Senator Simmons in his remarks during the debate:

> If we make a mistake and include in our designation of what is "income" something which is not income, but is **property**, then, of course, the court would come in and settle that controversy.[15]

---

[14] *Eisner v. Macomber*, 252 U.S. 189, 1920

[15] 1913 Congressional Record, Vol. L Part IV pg. 3845

CONSTITUTIONAL TAX STRUCTURE

(emphasis added)

How could income and property ever be confused? Again, it's obvious that the Senators are not referring to a house or a car when they say "property," but, in the context of income tax, it means the money one earns in a year. Numerous Supreme Court rulings can be cited to explain the distinction between income and principal, but citing *Eisner v. Macomber* (252 U.S. 189, 1920) is sufficient to establish the legal relationship between these two categories of money:

> "Income may be defined as the gain derived from capital, from labor, or from both combined," provided it be understood to include profit gained through a sale or conversion of capital assets.

Income is not simply "gain" or "profit," but *"gain derived from capital,"* which denotes financial gain from investment. This entire definition describes an investment gain. The Court rebuked the government for trying to expand the meaning of "income" by defining it as simply a financial "gain":

> The government, although basing its argument upon the definition as quoted, **placed chief emphasis upon the word "gain," which was extended to include a variety of meanings**; while the significance of the next three words was either overlooked or misconceived. "Derived from capital"; "the *gain derived from capital*," etc. Here, we have the essential matter.[16]
>
> **(emphasis added)**

---

[16] *Eisner,* supra

The Court concluded that income is

> *severed from* **the capital, however invested or employed**, and *coming in,* being *"derived"*—that is, *received* or *drawn by* the recipient (the taxpayer) for his *separate* use, benefit and disposal—*that* is income derived from property. **Nothing else answers the description.**[17]
>
> **(emphasis added)**

Income is severed from capital and it is derived from property—"nothing else answers the description"—but it cannot be the capital or the property itself. This decision defines "income" in the constitutional sense. "Income" is not a dictionary word or an economic term, since it now appears in the Constitution, and therefore "income," the same as "direct tax," requires a legal definition. Note 11 in *Commissioner v. Glenshaw Glass Co.* (348 U.S. 426, 1955) explains:

> In discussing § 61(a) of the 1954 Code, the House Report states:
>
> > "Section 61(a) provides that gross income includes 'all income from whatever source derived.' This definition is based upon the 16th Amendment, and the word 'income' is used in its constitutional sense."

And as Senator Cummins observed:

> When the people of the country granted to Congress the right to levy a tax on incomes, that right was granted with reference to the legal meaning and

---

[17] *Eisner,* supra

CONSTITUTIONAL TAX STRUCTURE

interpretation of the word "income" as it was then or as it might thereafter be defined or understood in legal procedure.[18]

"Income" in legal procedure is "gain derived from capital," which is legally separate from the capital itself, and this defines "income" in its constitutional sense.

Although the Court references "labor" in this definition, "gain derived from labor" also denotes an investment gain. The one who invests capital to hire labor is the one who derives income from that labor. One must first have capital before one can invest and before one may employ hired labor; as the Court said, income is gain "severed from the capital, however *invested* or *employed*."[19] Gain from hired labor produces income as described by the Court in *Stratton's Independence, Ltd. v. Howbert* (231 U.S. 399, 1913):

> But when a company is digging pits, sinking shafts, tunneling, drifting, stoping, drilling, blasting, and hoisting ores, it is employing capital and labor in transmuting a part of the realty into personalty, and putting it into marketable form. The very process of mining is, in a sense, equivalent in its results to a manufacturing process. And, however the operation shall be described, the transaction is indubitably "business" within the fair meaning of the Act of 1909, and the gains derived from it are properly and strictly the income from that business; for **"income" may be defined as the gain derived from capital, from**

---

[18] Congressional Record, Vol. L Part IV, pg. 3844

[19] *Eisner,* supra

45

> **labor, or from both combined, and here we have combined operations of capital and labor.**
>
> **(emphasis added)**

The company above derived income from its hired labor. Abraham Lincoln made the same observation in his First Annual Message:

> A few men own capital, and that few avoid labor themselves, and with their capital hire or buy another few to labor for them.

Capital is required to hire labor, and if the gain from hired labor exceeds the capital investment, the result is "gain derived from labor." Hired labor produces income, one's own labor creates capital.

Income is derived from a source, as stated by the Sixteenth Amendment and in the law, but the nature of the source has been elusive. The Sixteenth Amendment states:

> Congress shall have power to lay and collect taxes on incomes, **from whatever source derived**, without apportionment among the several States, and without regard to any census or enumeration.
>
> **(emphasis added)**

Section 61(a) of the Internal Revenue Code contains the same language:

> GENERAL DEFINITION: except as otherwise provided in this subtitle, gross income means all income **from whatever source derived**, including (but not limited to) the following items.

CONSTITUTIONAL TAX STRUCTURE

(emphasis added)

However, the Supreme Court's definition of "income" in *Eisner* provides the link between income and its source: "Income may be defined as the **gain derived from capital,** from labor, or from both combined." The verb "derived" is the common word in all three examples.

- Income is *derived* from a source.
- Income is *derived* from capital.

Therefore:

- SOURCE = CAPTIAL.

The word "source" in the law and the Sixteenth Amendment means "capital": capital is the source from which all income is derived. Substituting the Supreme Court's definition of "income" into 61(a) yields:

> "Gross income means all **(gain derived from capital)** from whatever source **[of capital]** derived..."
>
> **(emphasis added)**

The verb "derived" is the key to understanding section 61(a). A thing is not derived from itself. The thing derived is transformed from the source into something different. To illustrate, consider if a statute read:

> Fruit juice means all juice from whatever source derived.

47

Is the "source" a source of juice or a source of fruit? Juice is not derived from itself so juice cannot be derived from juice. Juice is derived from fruit. The "source" is a source of fruit, and if there is no fruit, there can be no juice. If juice is derived from an apple, is the apple itself juice? Of course not. The apple is the source of fruit from which the juice is derived. In order to derive juice from an apple, it must be squeezed and processed—action is required to derive the juice. This analysis can be used to examine section 61(a):

Gross income means all income from whatever source derived.

Is the "source" a source of income or a source of capital? Income is not derived from itself, so income cannot be derived from income. Income is derived from capital. The "source" is a source of capital, and if there is no capital, there can be no income. If income is derived from employment earnings, are the employment earnings income? Of course not. The employment earnings are the source of capital from which the income is derived. In order to derive income from employment earnings, a portion of those earnings must be invested and result in a realized gain. Income is the gain derived from invested employment earnings or the "gain derived from capital."

Because of the use and meaning of the verb "derived" in the statute, there can be no "source of income" in a legal sense; income is derived ***from the source***. Thus, there are only "sources of capital." If "source" meant "source of income" it would render 61(a) logically, grammatically, and economically absurd:

> "Gross income means all income from whatever source **[of income]** derived…"

CONSTITUTIONAL TAX STRUCTURE

Income is not derived from income. Income is derived from capital, but the capital may originate from many different sources: any job, trade, occupation, or profession whatsoever is a source of capital.

<u>Labor creates capital and investments produce income:</u>

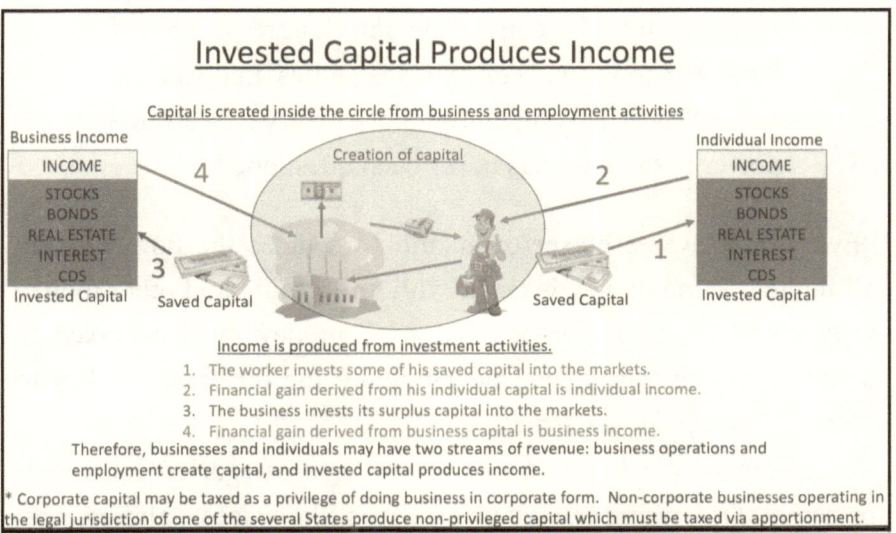

Therefore, one must have capital first before one can acquire *gain derived from capital*. It does not matter where the capital originates, and it does not matter how that capital is later invested or employed—any gain derived from that capital, whether the gain comes from investment or hired labor, is defined as income. Capital must be invested to produce income; juxtaposing the terms income and principal, it is obvious that "income" is an investment term. If one invests capital in the stock market, hired laborers, or a Picasso painting and receives a gain, that gain is income. Income is financial gain derived from all types of investments. Income—the gain derived from capital—is the other constitutional category of money.

D. Taxing Principal and Income

Congress can tax everything. There is no object and there is no activity that Congress cannot tax. The only stipulation is HOW a thing taxed. Is the object taxed with uniformity or with apportionment? Chief Justice White, in his *Brushaber* opinion, said:

> That the authority conferred upon Congress by § 8 of Article I "to lay and collect taxes, duties, imposts and excises" is exhaustive and embraces every conceivable power of taxation has never been questioned.[20]

"Every conceivable power of taxation" includes the power to tax all money. Some money is taxed with uniformity, and other money is taxed with apportionment, but ALL money must be taxed in one category or the other. Understanding the difference is key to comprehending the tax structure.

All money must fit into one of two legal categories: income or principal. Describing money using terms like wages, salaries, tips, commissions, etc., does not describe how money is taxed. Money gets taxed based on whether it is income or principal, and the legal distinction between income and principal must be strictly enforced because they are taxed differently in our dual system of government. This dual system of government is described not only by the Supreme Court, but also in Congressional debate:

> Under the dual system which prevails the bulk of the taxes imposed in the States are of the direct character. They are upon property; they are in some instances upon incomes; they are in more instances upon the estates of decedents, and in various ways they are of

---

[20] *Brushaber*, supra

the direct form. It is true that the Federal Government, generally speaking, imposes its taxes in an indirect form. **But when we come to consider the whole field of taxation, as divided between the two classes of government**, I undertake to say that a very much larger sum is raised from the direct form of taxation than from the indirect form.[21]

(emphasis added)

Because the field of taxation is divided between the two classes of government, the legal meaning of "income" is the basis for dividing financial resources between them because the legal distinction determines how money gets taxed. This legal distinction between income and principal explains why Senator Cummins said:

> When the people of the country granted to Congress the right to levy a tax on incomes, that right was granted with reference to the **legal meaning and interpretation of the word "income" as it was then or as it might thereafter be defined or understood in legal procedure.**[22]

(emphasis added)

The interpretation of "income," as understood in legal procedure, determines whether money is taxed with uniformity or with apportionment. "Income," as defined in legal procedure, cannot be **capital**—it cannot be money that is property. A tax on property, including money that is property, is a direct tax that must be apportioned, but an apportioned "income" tax is prohibited. The subjects of each tax are different:

---

[21] 1913 Congressional Record, Vol. L part IV pg. 3814

[22] Ibid, pg. 3843

51

> Whatever difficulty there may be about a precise and scientific definition of "income," it imports, as used here, something entirely distinct from principal or capital either as a **subject of taxation** or as a **measure of the tax**.[23]
>
> **(emphasis added)**

The subject of a tax on "income" is the *gain derived from capital*, but the subject of a tax on capital is the property created by one's own labor. A tax on capital is a tax on money that is property, but a tax on income is a tax on money that is profit. While Congress may tax income without apportionment, a direct tax on capital must be apportioned or Congress can't touch it because a tax on capital is a source of revenue the Constitution reserves to the States. Simply stated, unless Congress enacts an apportioned direct tax on capital, only the State can tax the employment earnings and business profits that her own citizens earn working in the State because that money is capital, it is principal, and it is property. All the capital that is created from employment and business activities within a State is a source of revenue the Constitution reserves to that State. For example, money in an employer's account is capital. When an employee is paid, capital is transferred from the business to the employee and capital is deposited into the employee's account. The money becomes the employee's property. In contrast, income is gain, it is profit, it is "severed from the capital however invested or employed."[24] The capital deposited into a worker's account will earn interest; this interest is "gain derived from capital" that can be taxed without apportionment because it is *one* type of "income." Congress may tax

---

[23] *Doyle,* supra

[24] *Eisner,* supra

CONSTITUTIONAL TAX STRUCTURE

all types of "income" without apportionment, but not the capital from which the "income" is derived. Taxing capital is a source of revenue the Constitution reserves to the States.

The IRS is desperate to suppress the idea of capital in individual finance. All money must be income so it can be taxed without apportionment. In the IRS universe, an employer deposits income into a worker's bank account, the income earns interest, and produces more income. Or, the worker invests income into the markets where it produces more income, so that income is derived from income. There is no capital in our capitalist economy. This is absurd. When a person or business makes money, it is capital; when money makes money, it is income.

Distinguishing between capital and income is one of the ways that the Constitution divides the power of taxation.

All money is taxed as either INCOME or PRINCIPAL:

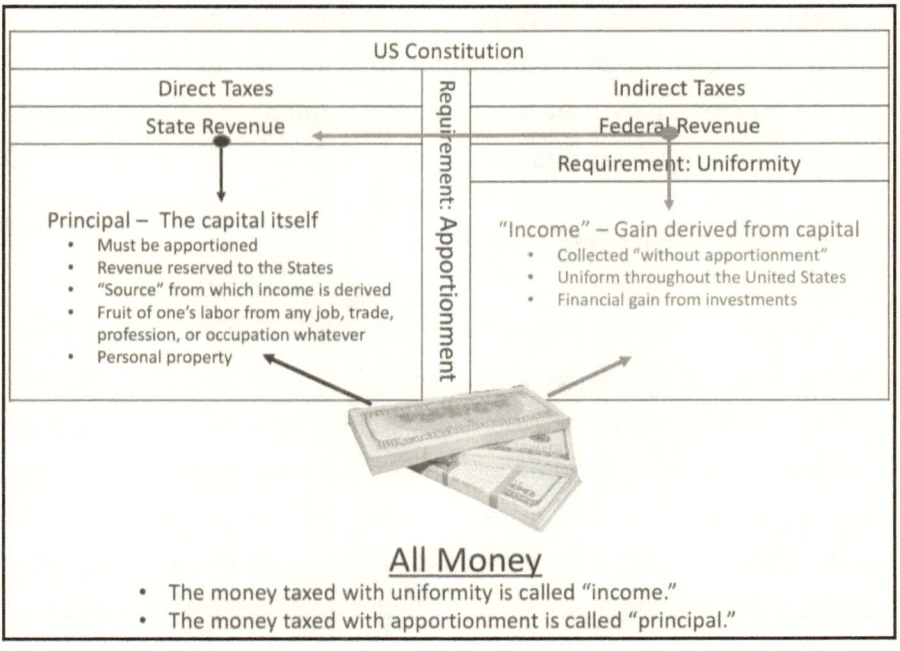

53

In the context of the Federal Income Tax, income and principal are not vague economic terms but precise legal terms because they are taxed differently and their legal definitions determine how financial resources are divided between the Federal and the State governments. The Constitution divides the taxing power into direct and indirect taxes and also divides financial resources between the State and Federal governments; this division requires that these terms be understood with legal precision. Money is taxed based on its legal character; its legal character determines whether the money is taxed with apportionment or with uniformity. The knowledge that some money is property and must be taxed as property is knowledge that the public has almost completely forgotten. Capital is financial gain that is created by business operations and employment activities; it is property and is taxed with apportionment. A tax on capital is a source of revenue the Constitution reserves to the States. "Income" is "gain derived from capital"; it is financial gain that comes from investments. "Income" is taxed with uniformity and is a primary source of revenue for the Federal government. The legal distinction is simple to comprehend: one works to create capital, and from invested capital, one derives income.

E. What Is "Gross Income?"

"Gross income" is a custom-defined legal term that combines a tax on "income" with special categories of capital that may be taxed indirectly. Although a tax on most capital is considered a direct tax that requires apportionment, taxes on privilege and license fees are examples of indirect taxes on capital that may be taxed with uniformity. The Federal Income Tax is not restricted to taxing only income, but it is restricted to taxes that are uniform throughout the

CONSTITUTIONAL TAX STRUCTURE

United States because there are no apportioned taxes in the Internal Revenue Code. Thus, "gross income" combines "income" (which is taxed with uniformity) with those special categories of capital which may also be taxed with uniformity. "Gross income" includes all financial gains that Congress may tax with uniformity, but it does not include any financial gains that must be taxed by apportionment.

The statutory definition of "gross income" is found in section 22(a) of the 1939 Internal Revenue Title, and also the Statues at Large, Vol. 52, Page 457, Chapter 289, Section 22(a), defined as:

> (a) GENERAL DEFINITION.—*"Gross income" includes gains, profits, and income derived from* salaries, wages, or compensation for personal service, of whatever kind and in whatever form paid, or from professions, vocations, trades, businesses, commerce, or sales, or dealings in property, whether real or personal, growing out of the ownership or use of or interest in such property; also from interest, rent dividends, securities, or the transaction of any business carried on for gain or profit, *or gains or profits and income derived from any source whatever.*
>
> **(emphasis added)**

In Title 26, the definition of "gross income" is found in section 61(a), which first appeared in the 1954 Internal Revenue Code, where it was defined as:

> GENERAL DEFINITION: except as otherwise provided in this subtitle, gross income means all income from whatever source derived, including (but not limited to) the following items:

(1) (Compensation for services, including fees, commissions, fringe benefits, and similar items;
(2) Gross income derived from business;
(3) Gains derived from dealings in property;
(4) Interest;
(5) Rents;
(6) Royalties;
(7) Dividends;
(8) Alimony and separate maintenance payments;
(9) Annuities;
(10) Income from life insurance and endowment contracts;
(11) Pensions;
(12) Income from discharge of indebtedness;
(13) Distributive share of partnership gross income;
(14) Income in respect of a decedent; and
(15) Income from an interest in an estate or trust.

The 1939 Internal Revenue Title was enacted into positive law on February 10, 1939. The Congressional Joint Committee on taxation said:

> The Internal Revenue Code of 1939, 53 Stat. (Part 1), 1, enacted on February 10, 1939, was the first reenactment into positive law of the general and permanent statues relating to internal revenue since the enactment of the Revised Statues in 1874. The Revised Statues (R.S.) were enacted into positive law and therefore, reference to the Statutes at Large is unnecessary.[25]

---

[25] Derivations of Code Sections of the Internal Revenue Codes of 1939 and 1954, Joint Committee on Taxation. Jan 21, 1992

CONSTITUTIONAL TAX STRUCTURE

By 1939, the Internal Revenue Statutes had not been enacted into positive law since 1874, and since 1939, no subsequent Internal Revenue Title, including Title 26, has ever been enacted into positive law. While the Internal Revenue Code (which is included in the Title) was amended in 1954 and again in 1986, amending the Code does not amend the underlying statutes from which the Code is derived; this has provoked some debate regarding which definition of "gross income" is the legal one. The House of Representatives' website explains the significance of positive law and non-positive law titles:

> The distinction is legally significant. Non-positive law titles are prima facie evidence of the law, but positive law titles constitute legal evidence of the law in all Federal and State courts (1 U.S.C. 204).

> Having, on one hand, non-positive law titles as prima facie evidence of the law, and on the other hand, positive law titles as legal evidence of the law, means that both types of titles contain statutory text that can be presented to a Federal or State court as evidence of the wording of the law. The difference between "prima facie" and "legal" is a matter of authoritativeness.

> Statutory text appearing in a non-positive law title may be rebutted by showing that the wording in the underlying statute is different. Typically, statutory text appearing in the Statutes at Large is presented as proof of the words in the underlying statute. The text of the law appearing in the Statutes at Large prevails

over the text of the law appearing in a non-positive law title.[26]

The 1939 Title is the positive-law Internal Revenue Title, while Title 26 is the non-positive-law Internal Revenue Title, and they are both in force concurrently. While they both contain a definition that is sufficient to prove the existence of "gross income" in the law, if the wording and legal meaning of the term is in dispute, the positive law definition overrides the non-positive law definition. The statutory definition of "gross income" is found in the 1939 Title as confirmed by the Supreme Court in *Commissioner v. Glenshaw Glass Co.* (348 U.S. 426, 1955). Note 11 in that case reads:

> In discussing § 61(a) of the 1954 Code, the House Report states:
>
> "This section corresponds to section 22(a) of the 1939 Code. While the language in existing section 22(a) has been simplified, the all-inclusive nature of statutory gross income has not been affected thereby. Section 61(a) is as broad in scope as section 22(a)."

Section 22(a) is still "existing," and has not been repealed or replaced, and it is self-evident that if the simplified language of section 61(a) does not affect statutory gross income, then 61(a) cannot be the statutory definition. The catchall provision of statutory gross income is described as "gains or profits and income derived from any source whatever":

---

[26] US House of Representatives Office of the Law Revision Counsel, UNITED STATES CODE website, http://uscode.house.gov/codification/legislation.shtml

CONSTITUTIONAL TAX STRUCTURE

> Such decisions demonstrate that we cannot but ascribe content to the **catchall provision** of § 22(a), "gains or profits and income derived from any source whatever." **The importance of that phrase has been too frequently recognized** since its first appearance in the Revenue Act of 1913 to say now that it adds nothing to the meaning of "gross income."[27]
>
> **(emphasis added)**

The catchall provision of 22(a) provides this functional definition and in 1955, the Supreme Court cited "the importance of that phrase" for the meaning of "gross income," even after section 61(a) was written into the 1954 Code. Additionally, in *Helvering v. Clifford* (309 U.S. 331, 1940), the Court explains the significance of this catchall language:

> The broad sweep of this language indicates the purpose of Congress to use the full measure of its taxing power **within those definable categories.**
>
> **(emphasis added)**

The definable categories of "gross income" are "gains or profits" and "income." Together, these categories represent a "catchall" for all financial gains. For those who appreciate formulas, the relationship can be expressed as a quantity with two variables:

Gross Income = (gains or profits) + (income derived from any source whatever)

---

[27] *Commissioner v. Glenshaw Glass Co.,* 348 U.S. 426, 1955

"Gains or profits" and "income" are separate financial gains, and "gross income" captures them both.

- The category "Gains or Profits" includes the creation of capital (its origin, its birth, its coming into existence for the first time), growth of existing capital and capital acquired from taxable privilege. Business operations and employment activities create capital. Market forces and making improvements may result in the increased value of existing capital. Taxable privilege involves advantageous use of the law, privileged employment positions, and licenses to pursue certain careers. Capital may be taxed either directly or indirectly. A direct tax on gains or profits must be apportioned, and an indirect tax on gains or profits must be uniform.
- The category "Income" includes the financial gain from investments—the "gain derived from capital." Interest, dividends, rents, fine art, collectibles, and investments of all kinds can produce income. All taxes on income must be uniform throughout the United States because the Sixteenth Amendment prohibits apportioned income taxes.

The full measure of Congress's taxing power describes the authority to enact both direct and indirect taxes, and this authority is independently applied within each category. This means Congress can impose direct taxes and indirect taxes on "gains or profits," and direct and indirect taxes on "income." Organizing this information makes it easier to understand.

Gross Income includes:

1. <u>Gains or profits</u>: Capital

    a. "Direct taxes" on gains or profits must be apportioned
    b. Indirect taxes on gains or profits must be uniform

2. <u>Income</u>: "Gain derived from capital"

    a. "Direct taxes" on "income" are prohibited by the Sixteenth Amendment.
    b. Indirect taxes on "income" must be uniform

The Supreme Court recognizes these categories of financial gain. The first example is from *Pollock v. Farmer's Loan and Trust*:

> We have considered the act only in respect of the tax on **income** derived from real estate, and from invested personal property, and have not commented on so much of it as bears on **gains or profits from business, privileges, or employments**, in view of the instances in which taxation on business, privileges, or employments has assumed the guise of an excise tax and been sustained as such.[28]
>
> **(emphasis added)**

"Income" is one category of financial gain and "gains or profits" is another. Another example of the Court's differentiation between these terms is found here:

---

[28] *Pollock*, supra

> The Act of 1913 contains no similar language, but, on the contrary, deals with dividends as a particular item of **income**, leaving them free from the normal tax imposed upon individuals, subjecting them to the graduated surtaxes only when received as dividends (38 Stat. 167, paragraph B), and subjecting the interest of an individual shareholder in the undivided **gains and profits** of his corporation to these taxes only in case the company is formed or fraudulently availed of for the purpose of preventing the imposition of such tax by permitting **gains and profits** to accumulate instead of being divided or distributed.[29]
>
> **(emphasis added)**

And the District Court also explained the distinction:

> The true function of the words "gains" and "profits" is to limit the meaning of the word "income" and to show its use only in the sense of receipts which constituted an accretion to capital.[30]

"Gains or profits" limit the meaning "income" because "income" only refers to the receipts over and above the capital, it cannot be the capital itself. If money is "gains or profits" it cannot be "income." Income is distinct from gains and profits; clearly, the Courts have recognized that "gross income" has two definable categories. It is important to note that the Sixteenth Amendment applies to taxes on "income" only —- the one category of "gross income" — the Amendment does not apply to capital.

---

[29] *Southern Pacific Co. v. Lowe, 247 US 330*

[30] *Southern Pacific Co. v. Lowe, 238 F 847 US District Court of New York*

CONSTITUTIONAL TAX STRUCTURE

"Gains or profits" describe capital. A direct tax on "gains or profits" is a direct tax on capital, and an indirect tax on "gains or profits" is an indirect tax on capital. A tax on business profits and employment earnings is a direct tax on capital, which requires apportionment. When rejecting the government's argument in *Eisner,* the Court gave the following explanation:

> Manifestly this argument must be rejected, since the amendment applies to income only, and what is called the stockholder's share in the accumulated profits of the company is capital, not income.[31]

Accumulated profits are *capital*, not income. Business owners should take note of that statement. This enlightening quote confirms that the Supreme Court differentiates between two categories of money: capital and income; that the Sixteenth Amendment applies to income only; and that accumulated profits (gains or profits) are capital not income. A tax on (non-corporate) business profits and employment earnings must be apportioned because that money is property.[32]

However, an indirect tax on "gains or profits" is an indirect tax on capital and is subject to the rule of uniformity like any other indirect tax. An indirect tax on "gains or profits" would include taxes on privilege and license fees, which can be taxed as an excise as described in *Flint v. Stone Tracy Co.* (220 U.S. 107, 1911):

> Excises are taxes laid upon the manufacture, sale, or consumption of commodities within the country,

---

[31] *Eisner,* supra

[32] Ever since the Corporate Tax Act of 1909 and the decision in *Flint v. Stone Tracy Co (1911),* a corporation's profits are subject to an excise tax for the privilege of doing business in a corporate capacity.

63

upon licenses to pursue certain occupations and upon corporate privileges; the requirement to pay such taxes involves the exercise of the privilege, and if business is not done in the manner described, no tax is payable.

And

...it is this privilege which is the subject of the tax, and not the mere buying, selling or handling of goods.

"Gains or profits" include taxes on privilege, as described by *Pollock,* which are indirect taxes on capital and must be included in the "gross income" calculation. Money that is earned by one's own effort is capital, but if that capital is acquired by privilege, it can be taxed as an excise because the privilege is the subject of the tax, not the capital. This qualifies as an indirect tax on capital. It might be more precise to state that the privilege is the subject of the tax and the capital is the measure of the tax; the more capital earned, the more tax one pays for the privilege. Such privileges might include federal employment as well as:

- Alimony
- Pensions
- Unemployment
- Inheritance
- Forgiveness of debt
- And others...

Alimony is a privilege. The law grants a person a judgement to squeeze a former spouse for money as part of a divorce settlement.

CONSTITUTIONAL TAX STRUCTURE

Alimony is the transfer of capital from one person to their former spouse. It is a financial gain, but the recipient did not work for it and thus it cannot be considered the conversion of a capital asset from one form to another. Alimony is a financial gain granted by law, which is interpreted as a privilege that may be taxed as an excise and must be included in the "gross income" calculation. Other privileges that allow a person to acquire money without working for it are "gross income" in the same way.

It could be argued that the "simplified" definition of "gross income" found in Section 61(a) exists to prevent modern readers from realizing that two separate financial gains are being taxed. "Gains or profits" is not specifically mentioned in the new language, and the reworded definition seems purposely composed to omit it, considering it has been present in every revenue act since 1862.[33] Camouflaging the specific reference to capital as a financial gain would make it easier to advance the idea that all money is income. Comparing the two definitions, it seems that "gains or profits" was edited out and replaced with specific examples of capital that may be taxed indirectly, like alimony, pensions, discharge of indebtedness, etc. Regardless, the language of 61(a) is irrelevant. If, as note 11 in the *Glenshaw* case states, section 61(a) is just as broad as 22(a), then it must tax financial gains from both capital and income or it would not be "as broad in scope as 22(a)." Therefore, 61(a) taxes "gains or profits and income" the same as 22(a) even if the "simplified" language is harder to decipher.

"Gross income" includes all money that Congress can tax using the rule of uniformity, including both "gains or profits" and "income."

---

[33] 1862 Income Duty; Statutes at Large Vol. 12, Page 473, Chapter 119, "SEC. 90. And be it further enacted, that there shall be levied, collected, and paid annually, upon the annual gains, profits, or income of every person residing in the United States."

BRIAN SWANSON

Excise taxes on income are taxes on the activities that produce income—investments of all kinds. Excise taxes on gains or profits are taxes on acquiring capital from a privileged activity and also include license fees. They are both taxed with uniformity. No money that must be taxed with apportionment is included in the "gross income" calculation (there is no money that is considered property) because apportioned taxes are paid by States, not by individuals. The Federal Income Tax is calculated using "gross income," which includes both income and that capital which may be taxed by the rule of uniformity. In contrast, the income tax is but one component of "gross income," which includes all financial gains that come from investments.

CONSTITUTIONAL TAX STRUCTURE

<u>All income is taxed with uniformity, but capital must be analyzed to determine if it is taxed with uniformity or with apportionment.</u>

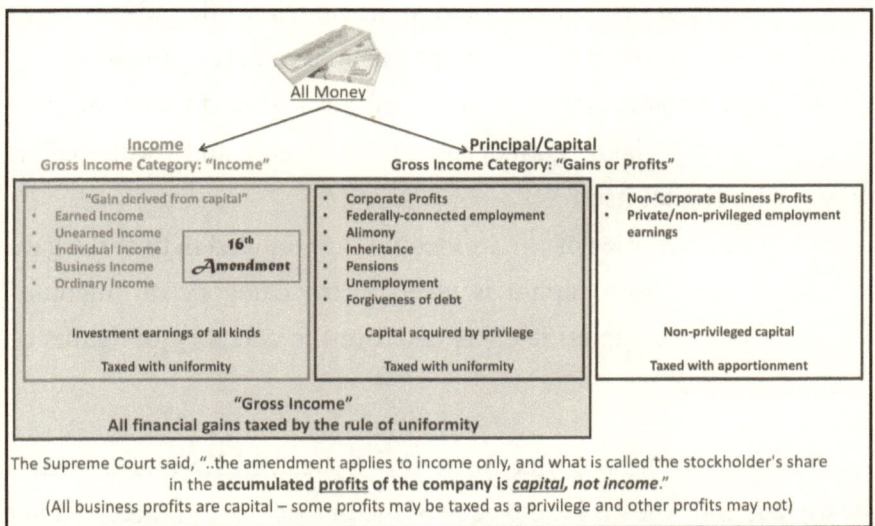

Capital is not subject to the limitations of the Sixteenth Amendment. The Amendment permits income to be taxed only by the rule of uniformity. However, capital is not subject to that limitation and may be taxed either with uniformity or with apportionment depending on the nature of the capital. Capital acquired by privilege may be taxed with uniformity because the capital is not the subject of the tax, but all other capital must be taxed by the rule of apportionment.

At this point in the book, the reader should have perceived a pattern. The Constitution has created a dual system of government such that most political and constitutional questions are divided in two.

- Political power is divided in two: the powers of Congress are delegated, and those powers not delegated are reserved to the States.

- The taxing power is divided in two: direct taxes are apportioned and indirect taxes are uniform.
- Financial resources are divided in two: direct taxes are a source of revenue reserved to the States, while indirect taxes are the Federal Government's primary source of revenue.
- The constitutional concept of money is divided in two: "income" is the gain derived from capital, and "principal" is the capital itself.
- The categories of "gross income" are divided in two: the gain derived from capital is taxed in the category of "income" while the capital itself is taxed in the category of "gains or profits."

The Constitutional Tax Structure is beautifully and logically designed, and when all the pieces of the puzzle are in place, it is not difficult to understand. The Federal Income Tax imposes taxes on both *capital* and *income*—don't be fooled by its name. In theory, "gross income" includes all financial gains, but after applying the Constitution's rules for taxation, it is reduced to all financial gains that Congress may tax with uniformity. "Direct taxes" are eliminated from the "gross income" calculation by the Sixteenth Amendment and the apportionment requirement, leaving only indirect taxes on "gains or profits" (capital) and indirect taxes on "income." "Taxable income" is what remains after deductions. When one speaks of the tax on income, or Income Tax, it only refers to that one component of "gross income," but the Federal Income Tax imposes indirect taxes on both capital and income.

CONSTITUTIONAL TAX STRUCTURE

<u>Logically equivalent statements:</u>

"Gains or profits" may be taxed either with apportionment or without apportionment. "Income" is only taxed without apportionment.

"Gains or profits" may be taxed either without uniformity or with uniformity. "Income" is only taxed with uniformity.

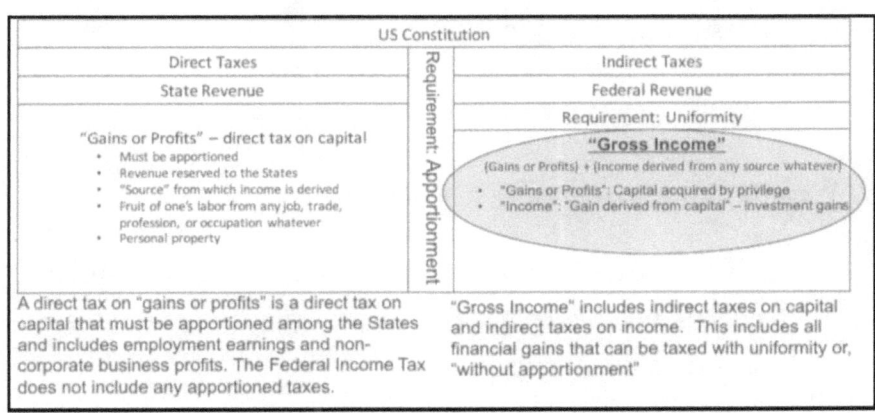

How to determine if money is taxable

1. Is the money in question income or principal? Is it the "gain derived from capital" or the capital itself?

   - If the money is "gain derived from capital" ("income"), it qualifies as "gross income"—pay the Federal Income Tax. (Indirect tax on activities that produce income apply to investments of all kinds.)

   - If the money is the capital itself, go to question 2.

2. Was the capital acquired by a privilege?

   - If "yes," the capital is taxable as an excise on "gains or profits" and thus qualifies as "gross income"—pay the Federal Income Tax (an indirect tax on capital).

   - If "no," the capital cannot be taxed by the Federal Income Tax because it is merely the conversion of a capital asset and thus the money is property, such as capital acquired from a typical paycheck. A tax on this capital would be a direct tax on "gains or profits" and would require apportionment (a direct tax on capital).

V. The Purpose and Meaning of the Sixteenth Amendment

A. Why Was It Adopted?

The Supreme Court's ruling in *Pollock v. Farmers' Loan & Trust Co.* (157 U. S. 429; 158 U. S. 601, 1895) altered the tax structure when it ruled that the tax on income from real estate and invested personal property must be considered a "direct tax" because the gains proceeded from property. A tax on income had never been ruled a "direct tax" before this decision because the capital (often called "invested personal property") and the income derived from it had always been considered separate from each other. The court reasoned that if the source of the income was the subject of a "direct tax," then the income derived from that source must also be the subject of a "direct tax." Personal property (money) and real estate were certainly the objects of a direct tax and thus a tax on income derived from them, said the Court, is also a direct tax. This is the origin of the "source" argument that was abolished in the Sixteenth Amendment. As a result of *Pollock,* taxation of all investment earnings required apportionment.

The ruling nullified the whole law, which had two parts: a tax on "income" and a tax on "gains or profits": a tax on the gain derived from capital and a tax on the capital itself. The Court said the tax on "gains or profits" was valid as an excise:

> We have considered the act only in respect of the tax on **income** derived from real estate, and from invested personal property, and have not commented on so much of it as bears on **gains or profits from business, privileges, or employments, in view of the instances in which taxation on business, privileges, or employments has assumed the guise of an excise tax** and been sustained as such.[34]
>
> **(emphasis added)**

An excise tax on business, privilege, or employment is an indirect tax on capital, but a direct tax on capital (business profits and employment earnings) would require apportionment. Additionally, the quote above illustrates how the tax on income and the tax on privilege are taxes on separate categories of gain. The tax on income required apportionment, but the tax on privileges did not. Though the excise tax on business, privilege, and employment was valid, the bulk of the revenue was intended to be raised from taxing income:

> It is evident that the income from realty formed a vital part of the scheme for taxation embodied therein. If that be stricken out, and also the income from all invested personal property, bonds, stocks, **investments of all kinds,** it is obvious that by far the largest part of the anticipated revenue would be eliminated, and this would leave the burden of the tax to be borne by professions, trades, employments,

---

[34] *Pollock*, supra

CONSTITUTIONAL TAX STRUCTURE

or vocations, and in that way what was intended as a tax on capital would remain in substance a tax on occupations and labor. We cannot believe that such was the intention of Congress[35]

(emphasis added)

The tax on income—gain from investments of all kinds—represented the greater part of the law's revenue, but was void, and the valid part of the law "would leave the burden of the tax to be borne by professions, trades, employments or vocations." It must be restated that the tax on employments and vocations was an excise tax in the form of privilege and license fees, and not a tax on earnings (or capital). Thus, the whole law was invalidated because the expected revenue from an excise on occupation and labor was so small as to be considered insignificant. The Court reasoned that one act could potentially combine an apportioned direct tax on income with an excise tax on business, privilege, and employment, but the law as written didn't qualify:

> We do not mean to say that an act laying by apportionment a direct tax on all real estate and personal property, or the **income** thereof, might not also lay excise taxes on **business, privileges, employments, and vocations**. But this is not such an act, and the scheme must be considered as a whole.[36]
>
> **(emphasis added)**

And since the law failed this test, the whole thing was declared void:

---

[35] *Pollock*, supra

[36] *Pollock*, supra

The tax imposed by sections twenty-seven to thirty-seven, inclusive, of the act of 1894, so far as it falls on the income of real estate and of personal property, being a direct tax within the meaning of the Constitution, and therefore unconstitutional and void because not apportioned according to representation, all those sections, constituting one entire scheme of taxation, are necessarily invalid.[37]

The tax on income required apportionment, but the indirect tax on capital in the form of an excise on "gains or profits from business, privilege, and employment" was sustained. From the beginning, the internal revenue laws have included an indirect tax on capital, but no internal revenue law has ever attempted to levy a direct tax on capital.

---

[37] *Pollock*, supra

CONSTITUTIONAL TAX STRUCTURE

<u>The *Pollock* decision split "gross income" and expanded the definition of "direct tax" to include income:</u>

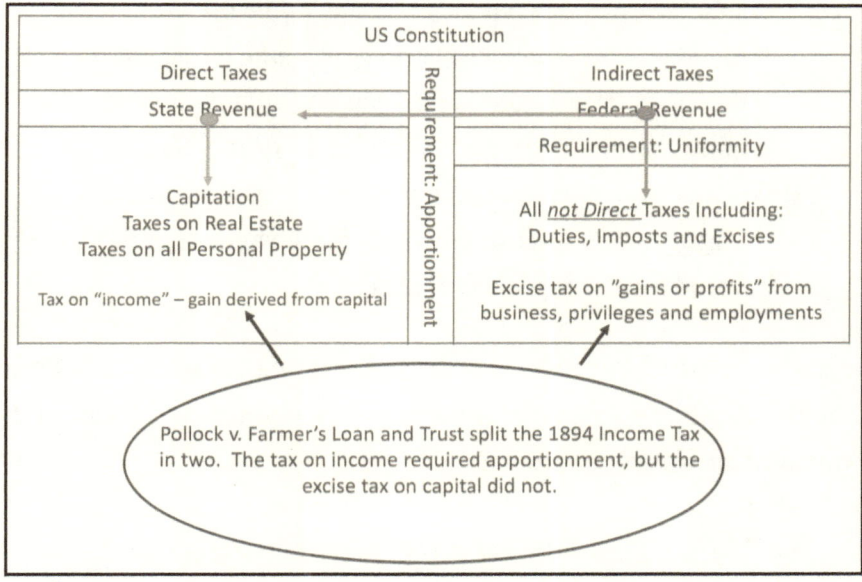

Dissenting judges and politicians condemned this ruling because it denied the national government necessary funding from a valid source. Not only was capital considered property, but after this ruling, the income derived from capital was also considered property. This had the effect of stripping this important source of revenue from the Federal Government and essentially giving it to the States. Many were angered. Justice Harlan, dissenting, said:

> Why do I say that the decision just rendered impairs or menaces the national authority? The reason is so apparent that it need only be stated. In its practical operation, this decision withdraws from national taxation not only all incomes derived from real estate, but tangible personal property, "invested, personal

75

property, bonds, stocks, investments of all kinds," and the income that may be derived from such property. This results from the fact that, by the decision of the court, all such personal property and all incomes from real estate and personal property, are placed beyond national taxation otherwise than by *apportionment* among the States *on the basis* simply *of population*. No such apportionment can possibly be made without doing gross injustice to the many for the benefit of the favored few in particular States.[38]

In order to bring revenue from investment earnings back within Congress's ability to tax it without apportionment, the Sixteenth Amendment was proposed.

B. What Did the Amendment Do?

The Sixteenth Amendment was ratified to reverse the *Pollock* decision, overturn the despised "source" reasoning, and restore all income taxes, regardless of the source, to the class of indirect taxes, which are collected without apportionment. The text:

The Congress shall have power to lay and collect taxes on incomes, from whatever source derived, without apportionment among the several states, and without regard to any census or enumeration.

The amendment makes no attempt to classify a tax on income as either a direct or indirect tax; if a reader assumes a such a classification, this is a flaw in the reader's logic. For those who understand logical

---

[38] *Pollock*, supra

CONSTITUTIONAL TAX STRUCTURE

reasoning, the amendment is written using the contrapositive and contains no language to suggest that the rules for taxation found in Article 1 have been amended or superseded, so creating a conditional statement from the Constitution's established rules results in the following:

- If the tax is direct, the tax is apportioned.

The contrapositive reads:

- If the tax is not apportioned, the tax is not direct.

The amendment did not change the rules: ***If income tax is not apportioned, then income tax is not a direct tax.*** If income tax is collected without apportionment, then it must be collected with uniformity, or it is an unconstitutional tax. An income tax collected with uniformity is logically equivalent to an income tax collected without apportionment—they both describe an indirect tax. Chief Justice White, in *Stanton v. Baltic Mining Co.* (1916), explains that:

> The Sixteenth Amendment conferred no new power of taxation, but simply **prohibited** the previous complete and plenary power of income taxation possessed by Congress from the beginning from being taken out of the category of indirect taxation to which it inherently belonged, and being placed in the category of direct taxation subject to apportionment by a consideration of the sources from which the income was derived.
> **(emphasis added)**

The Sixteenth Amendment prohibits income taxation from being taken out of the category of indirect taxation *to which it inherently belongs*. The tax on income must remain in the category of indirect taxation, where the Federal Government can tax it without apportionment. "Without apportionment" means "with uniformity," and uniformity is imposed "only on duties, imposts and excises,"[39] which are all indirect taxes.

<u>The Sixteenth Amendment overruled the expanded interpretation of "direct taxes" and reversed the split in "gross income" created by Pollock:</u>

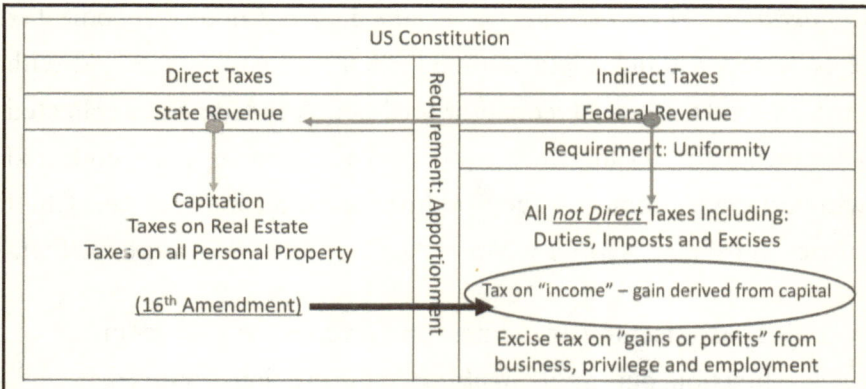

The amendment authorizes Congress to once again tax investment earnings without apportionment. "Income" has never been a reference to employment earnings. Treasury Department Legislative Draftsman F. Morse Hubbard, as quoted in the Congressional record, stated:

---

[39]   *Knowlton v. Moore*, supra

CONSTITUTIONAL TAX STRUCTURE

> The Sixteenth Amendment authorizes the taxation of income "from whatever source derived"—thus taking in **investment income**—"without apportionment among the several States." The Supreme Court has held that the Sixteenth Amendment did not extend the taxing power of the United States to new or excepted subjects but merely removed the necessity which might otherwise exist for an apportionment among the States of taxes laid on income whether it be derived from one source or another. So the amendment made it possible to bring **investment income** within the scope of a general income-tax law. It is still fundamentally an *excise* or *duty* with respect to the *privilege* of carrying on any *activity* or owning any property which produces income.[40]
>
> **(emphasis added)**

Investing capital is the activity targeted by the amendment, and ensuring that a tax on investment earnings will never again be ruled as a "direct tax" is its purpose. As stated earlier, Chief Justice Roberts provides a succinct and complete summary of "direct taxes":

> In 1895, we expanded our interpretation to include taxes on personal property and income from personal property, in the course of striking down aspects of the federal income tax (*Pollock v. Farmers' Loan & Trust Co.* 158 U.S. 601, 618, 1895). That result was overturned by the Sixteenth Amendment, although we continued to consider taxes on personal property

---

[40] 1943 Congressional Record, 78th Congress Vol. 89 Part 2, pg. 2580

to be direct taxes. (See *Eisner v. Macomber* 252 U.S. 189–219, 1920.)[41]

The effect of the Sixteenth Amendment is expressed in eight words: "that result was overturned by the Sixteenth Amendment." It did not exempt a direct tax from apportionment and it did not create a new tax. It overruled the expanded definition of "direct tax" and required that the tax on income now and forever remain in the category of indirect taxation, which is collected without apportionment.

The significance of income being categorized as an indirect tax is that it is voluntary; it does not indiscriminately fall upon every citizen, every worker, and every paycheck. One who chooses not to invest any capital will never pay an "income" tax. And one who neither invests any capital nor engages in any privileged employment activity will ever pay the Federal Income Tax.

---

[41] *NFIB v. Sibelius* (2012), supra

VI. The Non-Apportioned Direct Tax Myth

A. Origins

The idea that the Sixteenth Amendment gives Congress the power to enact an income tax as a non-apportioned direct tax is a myth used to conceal the true purpose of the amendment; this myth is found in history books, online resources, and even the IRS website:

> 16th Amendment
>
> In 1913, Wyoming ratified the 16th Amendment, providing the three-quarter majority of states necessary to amend the Constitution. The 16th Amendment gave Congress the authority to enact an income tax.[42]

The amendment did not give Congress the authority to enact an income tax. Congress always possessed that power under Article 1 Section 8, and it had taxed incomes numerous times, as *Brushaber* confirms:

---

[42] IRS Webpage: https://www.irs.gov/uac/brief-history-of-irs

The Sixteenth Amendment does not purport to confer power to levy income taxes in a generic sense, as that authority was already possessed.

The purpose of the myth is to confuse and distract the public so it does not learn that a constitutionally collected income tax is an indirect tax that does not apply to most Americans' employment earnings. Additionally, government agencies that describe an income tax as a direct tax exempt from the Constitution's apportionment requirement promote an insidious myth that threatens the Constitution's carefully designed tax structure. The IRS describes the income tax in this way on its website:

> Some individuals and groups assert that the Sixteenth Amendment does not authorize a direct non-apportioned income tax and, thus, U.S. citizens and residents are not subject to federal income tax laws.
>
> The Law: The constitutionality of the Sixteenth Amendment has invariably been upheld when challenged. Numerous courts have both implicitly and explicitly recognized that the Sixteenth Amendment authorizes a non-apportioned direct income tax on United States citizens and that the federal tax laws are valid as applied.[43]

Yet a non-apportioned direct tax is a contradiction that cannot exist within the tax structure.

---

[43] IRS webpage: https://www.irs.gov/tax-professionals/the-truth-about-frivolous-tax-arguments-section-i-d-to-e#_Toc350157906

A few lower court rulings such as *United States v. Collins* (920 F.2d 619, 629, 10th Cir. 1990), *In re Becraft* (885 F.2d 547, 548-49, 9th Cir. 1989), *Lovell v. United States* (755 F.2d 517, 518-20, 7th Cir. 1984), and others have supported this contradiction. To the extent that these lower court rulings describe income tax as a non-apportioned direct tax, they do so in defiance of *Brushaber v. Union Pacific R. Co.* (1916) and in open rebellion against a unanimous Supreme Court.

B. Unlimited Tax

A non-apportioned "direct tax" would be an unlimited tax subject to neither the rule of apportionment nor the rule of uniformity and would make the American public vulnerable to unlimited abuse and financial ruin. A direct tax is not constitutionally limited by uniformity,[44] so if a direct tax is exempted from apportionment, it becomes a tax without limitation. An unlimited income tax might result in taxpayers who earn the same income being taxed at varied rates, or citizens of the various States being taxed differently. Chief Justice White, writing for the unanimous *Brushaber* Court, passed his disapproving judgment on the idea that the Sixteenth Amendment authorizes such a thing as a "direct tax" without apportionment:

> But it clearly results that the proposition and the contentions under it, if acceded to, would cause one provision of the Constitution to destroy another; that is, they would result in bringing the provisions of the Amendment exempting a direct tax from

---

[44] *Knowlton v. Moore* (178 US 41, 1900): "Thus, the qualification of uniformity is imposed not upon all taxes which the Constitution authorizes, but only on duties, imposts and excises." *Brushaber v. Union Pacific RR* (240 US 1, 1916): "… the rule of uniformity, as such rule only applies to taxes which are not direct…"

> apportionment **into irreconcilable conflict** with the general requirement that all direct taxes be apportioned. Moreover, the tax authorized by the Amendment, being direct, would not come under the rule of uniformity applicable under the Constitution to other than direct taxes, and **thus it would come to pass that the result of the Amendment would be to authorize a particular direct tax not subject either to apportionment or to the rule of geographical uniformity, thus giving power to impose a different tax in one state or states than was levied in another state or states.** This result, instead of simplifying the situation and making clear the limitations on the taxing power, which obviously the Amendment must have been intended to accomplish, **would create radical and destructive changes in our constitutional system** and multiply confusion.
>
> **(emphasis added)**

The unanimous Court warns that the existence of a non-apportioned "direct tax" results in "irreconcilable conflict" and would "create radical and destructive changes" to our tax structure and constitutional system because "non-apportioned" can only mean "uniform," but a uniform direct tax cannot exist as *Knowlton v. Moore* and *Brushaber v. Union Pacific RR* have clearly ruled. Therefore, a non-apportioned direct tax is a contradiction outside the boundaries of the Constitutional Tax Structure because it would be subject to neither apportionment nor uniformity.

Had the Amendment proposed to authorize a tax requiring neither apportionment nor uniformity, it would have created

CONSTITUTIONAL TAX STRUCTURE

something new that the Constitution does not recognize or allow: a tax without limitation, hence the "radical and destructive change." The Amendment was not written to create a new tax or to alter the existing tax structure. White is so emphatic that he revisits this erroneous idea a second time:

> We are of opinion, however, that the confusion is not inherent, but rather arises from the conclusion that the Sixteenth Amendment provides for a hitherto unknown power of taxation—**that is, a power to levy an income tax which, although direct, should not be subject to the regulation of apportionment** applicable to all other direct taxes. And the far-reaching effect of this **erroneous assumption** will be made clear by generalizing the many contentions advanced in argument to support it.

For the hopelessly obtuse, he explains for a third time his unequivocal contempt for the non-apportioned "direct tax":

> Second, that the contention **that the Amendment treats a tax on income as a direct tax although it is relieved from apportionment** and is necessarily therefore not subject to the rule of uniformity, as such rule only applies to taxes which are not direct, *thus destroying the two great classifications which have been recognized and enforced from the beginning,* **is also wholly without foundation…**
> **(emphasis added)**

The contention that the Sixteenth Amendment treats the income tax as a direct tax but relieved from apportionment is "erroneous" and "wholly without foundation." White concluded that treating income tax as a direct tax without apportionment would result in "destroying the two great classifications [of tax] which have been recognized and enforced from the beginning." The Constitution's carefully designed tax structure would be destroyed if the amendment permitted an income tax to be imposed without limitation as a direct tax without apportionment. In *Brushaber,* the Chief Justice declares not once, not twice, but three times that a non-apportioned direct tax is constitutionally impossible.

<u>A non-apportioned direct tax would "create radical and destructive changes" and represents "irreconcilable conflict":</u>

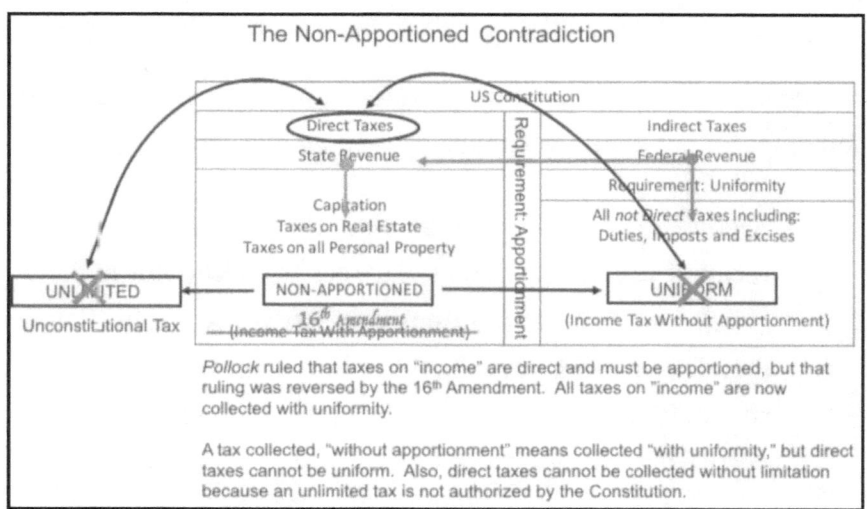

C. Lower Courts in Revolt

The clear judgment of the US Supreme Court has not prevented lower courts from directly contradicting the High Court's rulings. This rebellion of the lower courts undermines the integrity of the US justice system and threatens the public's confidence in the rule of law. For example, the Fifth Circuit has ruled:

> The Supreme Court promptly determined in *Brushaber v. Union Pacific Ry. Co.* (240 U.S. 1, 36 S.Ct. 236, 60 L.Ed. 493, 1916) that the Sixteenth Amendment provided the needed constitutional basis for the imposition of a direct non-apportioned income tax.[45]

Did the judges in the Fifth Circuit read *Brushaber?* The Jolly Roger is also flying proudly over the Eighth Circuit in clear defiance of the High Court in this ruling:

> Constitutional argument.
>
> Francisco's challenge is premised upon two theories: (1) **the income tax is an indirect tax**; and (2) income received in exchange for labor or services is not income within the meaning of the Sixteenth Amendment.
>
> The cases cited by Francisco clearly establish that the income tax is a direct tax, thus refuting the argument based upon his first theory. (See *Brushaber v. Union Pacific Railroad Co.* 240 U.S. 1, 19, 36 S. Ct. 236, 242, 60 L. Ed. 493, 1916.) (**The purpose of the Sixteenth**

---

[45] *Parker v. Comm'r,* 724 F.2d 469, 5th Cir., 1984

> Amendment was to take the income tax "out of the class of excises, duties and imposts and place it in the class of direct taxes.")[46]
>
> **(emphasis added)**

This ruling is treason. Not only does it contradict the High Court, but it also intentionally inverts its opinion. In *Brushaber,* the Court "recognized the fact that taxation on income was in its nature an excise entitled to be enforced as such," which the Eighth Circuit clearly contradicts. Then it inverts this decision in *Stanton*, which says that the purpose of the Sixteenth Amendment is to prohibit Congress's power of income taxation "from being taken out of the category of indirect taxation to which it inherently belonged." Our legal system is being perverted in order to protect the Internal Revenue Service as it illicitly taxes capital without apportionment and pilfers state treasuries.

The Tenth Circuit is doing more damage to the country than Robert E. Lee's army by destroying the public's confidence in the rule of law with this defiant ruling:

> Dickstein's argument **that the Sixteenth Amendment does not authorize a direct, non-apportioned tax on United States citizens similarly is devoid of any arguable basis in law.** Indeed, the Ninth Circuit recently noted "the patent absurdity and frivolity of such a proposition" (*in re Becraft*, 885 F.2d 547, 548, 9th Cir., 1989.) For seventy-five years, **the Supreme Court has recognized that the Sixteenth Amendment authorizes a direct non-apportioned**

---

[46] *United States v. Francisco*, 614 F.2d 617, 8th Cir., 1980

CONSTITUTIONAL TAX STRUCTURE

tax upon United States citizens throughout the nation, not just in federal enclaves (see *Brushaber v. Union Pac. R.R.*, 240 U.S. 1, 12-19, 36 S.Ct. 236, 239-42, 60 L.Ed. 493, 1916); **efforts to argue otherwise have been sanctioned as frivolous**, see, e.g., *Becraft*, 885 F.2d at 549.[47]

(emphasis added)

The Supreme Court has **NOT** recognized that the Sixteenth Amendment authorizes a direct non-apportioned tax! A third-grader could comprehend that the Supreme Court has declared that exempting a direct tax from apportionment "would create radical and destructive changes in our constitutional system." These rulings are doing as much damage to the credibility of our judicial system as the non-apportioned direct tax is doing to our federal system of government.

Not only are some lower courts in open rebellion, but Americans who rely on the Supreme Court's written opinions in federal court are being fined for frivolous arguments. It seems that in some lower courts, the written opinion of the Supreme Court is frivolous. What has happened to the intellectual integrity of our jurists? Have we become North Korea? If American citizens cannot rely on the written opinion of the Supreme Court when making a legal argument, then what good is the Supreme Court?

The open defiance of lower courts and the Internal Revenue Service, as they advance opinions in direct contradiction to the opinions of the U.S. Supreme Court, cannot be explained.

---

[47] *United States v. Collins* (920 F.2d 619, 10th Cir., 1990)

VII. Why Americans Pay Too Much Federal Income Tax

A. Legal Legerdemain and Terms of Art

Too many Americans do their Federal Income Taxes incorrectly. When Americans report the money that they are paid for their own labor on their Federal Income Tax form, they wrongly report their capital as income. Has any reader ever been cautioned that when doing their Federal Income Taxes, they should carefully separate the money that is capital from the money that is income? Do economists, tax consultants, and accountants advise Americans to distinguish between their capital and income when doing their taxes? Do Americans even know how to distinguish capital from income, or do they believe that all money they receive is income? When Americans report their capital as income, two errors occur: first, they pay a tax that they do not owe, and second, the Internal Revenue Service steals from the State governments their constitutionally protected source of revenue by taxing capital without apportionment.

The relationship between capital and income is elementary: One works to create capital, and from invested capital, one derives income—it's simple. It only becomes complicated when taxing authorities, through craft and subterfuge, attempt to tax capital as

CONSTITUTIONAL TAX STRUCTURE

though it were income. *Eisner* describes how revenue agents have been in the business of confusing these ideas for some time:

> The government, although basing its argument upon the definition as quoted, **placed chief emphasis upon the word "gain," which was extended to include a variety of meanings**; while the significance of the next three words was either overlooked or misconceived. "Derived from capital"; "the *gain derived from capital*," etc. Here, we have the essential matter.
>
> **(emphasis added)**

Adopting a variety of meanings for "gain" in an effort to tax capital as if it were income is not new. Creating capital is a financial gain, but it is not income. The Service may attempt to describe capital using terms of art found deep within the bowels of the Internal Revenue Code such as "wages," "salaries," or "gain," but these terms do not have the power to transform the legal character of money. Referring to capital as "earned income" does not legally transform capital into income. As the Court said in *Eisner:*

> It becomes essential to distinguish between what is and what is not "income," as the term is there used, and to apply the distinction, as cases arise, according to truth and substance, without regard to form.

Americans must understand the meaning of "income" according to truth and substance, and apply it to their own financial circumstances, and resist the Service's use of form and rhetorical deception. The meanings of many terms have been altered to confuse modern

Americans. Consider these examples from the 1913 Congressional debates on the income tax:

> Mr. CRAWFORD. I should like to ask the Senator if he seriously asserts that politicians have an income?
>
> Mr. WILLIAMS. Well, after they get through with the year they have not much left. [Laughter.]
>
> Mr. BRANDEGEE. No net income.
>
> Mr. WILLIAMS. **But they have at least had a _salary_ and an opportunity to have an _income_.**[48]

This exchange makes little sense today, considering the way these terms are confused. Today, "salary" and "income" have become synonyms, whereas in the exchange above, the salary represents capital, and depending how that capital might be invested, would give a senator the *opportunity to have an income.* The salary is not income. This observation from Senator Lodge is similar:

> Of course the men of **small _earnings_ and small _incomes_** pay taxes to the Government of the United States in the indirect form.[49]

Here is another example of how the proper distinction in terms has been obliterated. As in the above example, "earnings" and "incomes" have also become synonyms although, according to truth and substance, "earnings" are capital.

---

[48] 1913 Congressional Record, p. 3838, supra

[49] Ibid, p. 3839

CONSTITUTIONAL TAX STRUCTURE

So while confusion and the use of alternate terms to describe money do not have the power to legally transform capital into income, they do have the power to confuse the public, tricking them into erroneously reporting their capital as income and then paying a tax they do not owe. Considering the terms in use today, the only income that is truly "income," according to truth and substance and the Sixteenth Amendment, is what we call "unearned income"—the gain derived from capital. The correct legal and constitutional term for what we call "earned income" is **capital.** The IRS has changed the terms. Congress and the Supreme Court agree that the two categories of money are income and principal, but the IRS refers to these categories as "unearned income" and "earned income." Referring to capital as "earned income" is an attempt to obliterate the distinction between income and principal by using adjectives, modifiers, semantics, and terms of art.

Another opportunity for confusion exists in name of the tax itself: The Federal Income Tax. The name of the tax has no relationship to the operation of the tax; it is mostly a public relations gambit like the *Affordable Care Act* and the *Patriot Act*, which many believed were neither affordable nor patriotic. It's just a name. One may have no "income" in the constitutional sense—no gain derived from capital—and still owe Federal Income Tax. If one has no "income" yet does have taxable "gains or profits," then that person still has "gross income" and must calculate a tax liability and pay the Federal Income tax. The Federal Income Tax imposes indirect taxes on both capital and income regardless of what its name might suggest.

This is the part of the Code that is deliberately misleading. The terms of art used in the Code and their meanings are meant to confuse the public so that they unwittingly report their capital as income.

B. What Is Entered on Line 7 of a 1040?

Americans wrongly report their capital as income because they do not understand the terms that are used in the law. Term confusion is how the establishment, the bureaucrats, and the administrators take advantage of an ignorant public. Most people and most business owners have never read a single section of the Internal Revenue Code. They are encouraged not to read it and instead are persuaded to simply heed the advice and counsel of the experts. They do this at their own financial peril. The Ninth Circuit Court of Appeals, in *Lavin v. Marsh* (644 f.2d 1378, 1981), warns:

> Persons dealing with the government are charged with knowing government statutes and regulations, and they assume the risk that government agents may exceed their authority and provide misinformation.

When doing taxes, we are all "dealing with the government." Everybody must read and understand the statutes for themselves so they will know if a government agent is acting outside the law or providing false information. While it may be daunting and impractical in many cases, special attention to these revenue statutes ought to be regularly rehearsed because taxes affect every American's finances and freedom.

Americans are instructed to report their "wages" on line 7 of the form 1040. Those who have never read the legal definition of "wages" in the Internal Revenue Code have no idea what it means. It does not mean the same as the word found in the dictionary. "Wages" are paid to a privileged class of worker who pay an excise tax for working in their privileged position. "Wages" is a term of art that

CONSTITUTIONAL TAX STRUCTURE

has a compound definition found in Section 3401(a) of the Internal Revenue Code. It reads:

> For purposes of this chapter, the term "<u>wages</u>" means all remuneration (other than fees paid to a public official) **for services performed by an employee for his** employer, including the cash value of all remuneration (including benefits) paid in any medium other than cash...
>
> **(emphasis added)**

"Wages," as defined, are paid to an "employee." "Employee" is then defined later in the section under paragraph (c):

> For purposes of this chapter, the term "employee" includes an officer, employee, or elected official of the United States, a State, or any political subdivision thereof, or the District of Columbia, or any agency or instrumentality of any one or more of the foregoing. The term "employee" also includes an officer of a corporation.

BRIAN SWANSON

"WAGES" are paid to "employees" who are defined as a very small group of people who have accepted employment that maybe taxed by Federal authority.

---

§ 3401(a)

Wages For purposes of this chapter, the term "wages" means all remuneration (other than fees paid to a public official) for services performed by an **employee** for his employer,......etc, etc.

(c) **Employee**
For purposes of this chapter, the term "employee" includes an officer, employee, or elected official of the United States, a **State**, or any political subdivision thereof, or the District of Columbia, or any agency or instrumentality of any one or more of the foregoing. The term "employee" also includes an officer of a corporation.

§ 7701 **(10) State**
The term "State" shall be construed to include the District of Columbia, where such construction is necessary to carry out provisions of this title.

The first thing the rational mind will perceive is that "employee" is not defined as "every person from sea to shining sea in every job, trade, profession, or occupation who gets a paycheck." "Employee" is a very carefully and narrowly defined term of art used to describe those who have accepted work in a privileged position that may be taxed under the excise authority of the United States. The money paid to every "employee" is legally defined as "wages" that can be taxed as an excise tax on the privilege of working in one of the positions described. Numerous courts have said that the use of the term "includes" does not exclude all others not listed,[50] but it does not include all others either: it clearly includes some and excludes others. This means not every privileged job is listed in 3401(c), but rather it lists the types of jobs

---

[50]   *US v. Latham*, 754 F.2d 750

CONSTITUTIONAL TAX STRUCTURE

that qualify as a privilege. Therefore, "employees" who earn "wages" describes all people who have accepted an employment position that can be taxed under the excise authority of the United States, such as members of the military and railroad workers who are also "employees" who earn "wages," even though they are not specifically listed. Knowing whether you work in one of these privileged positions is one piece of the puzzle needed to do federal taxes correctly.

In *McCulloch v. Maryland* (17 U.S. 316, 1819), the Supreme Court defined the limits of a state's taxing authority to be co-extensive with its jurisdiction:

> It may be objected to this definition, that the power of taxation is not confined to the people and property of a state. It may be exercised upon every object brought **within its *jurisdiction*.** This is true, but to what source do we trace this right? It is obvious, that it is an **incident of sovereignty, and is *co-extensive* with that to which it is an incident. All subjects over which the sovereign power of a state extends, are objects of taxation; but those over which it does not extend, are, upon the soundest principles, exempt from taxation. This proposition may almost be pronounced self-evident.**
>
> The sovereignty of a state extends to everything which exists by its own ***authority***, or is introduced by its ***permission***.
>
> **(emphasis added)**

In this case, every example of an "employee" listed in 3401(c) either works within the Federal Government's legal jurisdiction or in a

97

position created by the Federal Government's own authority (or introduced by its permission), and all these people earn "wages." Working for the Federal Government is a taxable activity according to the Supreme Court in United States v. County of Allegheny (322 U.S. 174, 1944):

> The "Government" is an abstraction, and its possession of property largely constructive. Actual possession and custody of Government property nearly always are in someone who is not himself the Government, but acts in its behalf and for its purposes. He may be an officer, an agent, or a contractor. His personal advantages from the relationship by way of salary, profit, or beneficial personal use of the property may be taxed, as we have held.

For example, any private employer doing business in D.C. (or any other federal jurisdiction), federal employees, corporate officers, railroad employees, and other federal instrumentalities can all be taxed under the excise authority of the United States. The list of "employees" is potentially endless. However, the typical butcher, baker, and candlestick maker—or business owner—who works in the legal jurisdiction of one of the Fifty States are not "employees" as defined and do not earn "wages" as defined. Their earnings are not reported on line 7 because their money is capital that was not acquired by any personal advantage connected to the Federal Government, or other privilege, that may be taxed as an excise.

"Wages" are capital because they are compensation for individual labor and are classified as "gains or profits." But "wages" are capital that has been acquired by privilege, and a tax on "wages"

CONSTITUTIONAL TAX STRUCTURE

represents an indirect tax on capital because the privilege is the subject of the tax, not the capital itself. Like alimony and other taxes on privilege, "wages" qualify as capital that may be taxed by the rule of uniformity, and must be included in the "gross income" calculation. "Wages" are reported on line 7 of form 1040 for those who are paying an excise tax on the privilege of working in an employment position that exists because of federal authority. For those who accept federally-connected employment, both their capital (employment earnings) and their income (investment earnings) are subject to the Federal Income Tax. However, the vast majority of Americans do not earn "wages," so only their income is subject to the Federal Income Tax, not their capital because their employment earnings cannot be taxed under the excise authority of the United States. Americans are encouraged to misunderstand this term and imagine that the term "wages" as defined in the law is defined the same way as it is in the dictionary. Americans must read the Code to comprehend the distinction, because the experts upon whom we are encouraged to rely either won't explain it or don't understand it themselves. Remember, O reader: You are charged with knowing the statutes, and if a government official misleads you, it's your fault for not knowing them.

This is one example of a term of art contained in the Code, yet there are many more legal terms in the Internal Revenue Code that do not mean what most people suppose they mean. This confusion is intentional.

C. The Trap

The Internal Revenue Code is misunderstood. Its administrators prefer confusion because the trillions of dollars that flow into the Federal Treasury wouldn't be there if the Code were properly understood. Its administrators have a great advantage in perpetuating this misunderstanding, considering the criminal lack of basic economic education among the current generation of Americans. This scheme would never work if Americans simply understood the difference between capital and income. But they do not. Americans are deceived each year when they receive their W2 forms from their employers declaring that the money they earned with their own labor qualifies as "wages" and is subject to the Federal Income Tax.

Employers do not read the law any more closely than the public. In one sense, it's not the employers' fault, but on the other hand, it is everyone's fault. We are all responsible for understanding the law, but we do not. And the employers are just as afraid of the IRS as everyone else. So, when the IRS commands every employer to issue W2s to their employees, they do so without complaint, without knowing what the terms mean, and without knowing to whom the W2 applies. Who wants to challenge the IRS?

However, the law clearly states that W2s are only to be issued to "employees" who earn "wages" as defined in the law. If a person does not qualify under that definition, no money should be withheld and no W2 should be issued. This is how Americans get hooked, because most Americans do not qualify for a W2 under that definition, but they do not know it. Additionally, they do not know how to respond to a W2 that was wrongly issued. Section 6051 reads, in part:

Receipts for Employees (W2)

(a) REQUIREMENT Every person required to deduct and withhold from an employee a tax under section 3101 or 3402...shall furnish to each such employee

CONSTITUTIONAL TAX STRUCTURE

in respect of the remuneration paid by such person to such employee during the calendar year, on or before January 31 of the succeeding year...a written statement showing the following:

(1) the name of such <u>person,</u>
(2) the name of the <u>employee</u> (and an identifying number for the <u>employee</u> if wages as defined in <u>section 3121(a)</u> have been paid),
(3) **the total amount of <u>wages</u> as defined in section 3401(a),**
(4) the total amount deducted and withheld as <u>tax</u> under section 3402,
(5) **the total amount of <u>wages</u> as defined in section 3121(a)**

         (emphasis added)

Again, rational minds will immediately notice that "Every person required to deduct and withhold" doesn't identify *who* is required to deduct and withhold. Apparently, these special people know who they are, because it doesn't say "Every employer is required to deduct and withhold." Additionally, only "wages as defined in section 3401(a)" (or 3121[a]) should be reported on a W2, but unfortunately for most Americans, what is actually reported on their W2s is the capital they created with their own labor that can only be taxed by apportionment. Therefore, no W2 should be issued to most Americans because their money isn't "wages as defined in 3401(a)." Unfortunately, once a W2 is issued, it creates a legal presumption that the person identified on the form has received money that qualifies for the tax. This is how people who do not owe the tax become liable for it unless the erroneous documents are challenged and refuted.

Those who are actually required to deduct and withhold can be found in section 3402:

> Income Tax Collected at the source
>
> **(a) Requirement of withholding**
>
> **(1) In general** Except as otherwise provided in this section, every employer making payment of wages shall deduct and withhold upon such wages a tax determined in accordance with tables or computational procedures prescribed by the Secretary.

So here it can be seen how these legal terms are carefully woven into the law. Only those employers making a "payment of wages" shall deduct and withhold—not every employer who pays their workers money. "Wages" have already been defined, and the reader should understand that "wages" are privileged earnings.

Unfortunately, Americans who never become familiar with the Code or the Constitution do not know to whom a W2 should be issued or why. Thus, they cannot identify when a W2 has been issued in error. This misunderstanding has been so well inculcated into the American conscience over the generations that any truth that might correct the common misunderstanding is greeted with suspicion.

A. How to Respond to an Erroneous W2

A complete and comprehensive analysis of how the income tax law operates, how to correct errors, and how to present testimony

CONSTITUTIONAL TAX STRUCTURE

regarding the truth of one's own financial transactions has been presented by Peter Hendrickson in his book *Cracking the Code.* An exhaustive analysis of the law and references that can help one submit correct tax returns can further be found on his website: losthorizons.com. What is presented in this section is a very brief summary based on that work.

It is the individual's responsibility to recognize if the money reported on a W2 is correct or not. The individual must be able to distinguish between their capital and their income, and also know if the capital they earned is from a privileged position that may be taxed as an excise. The employer does not have the power to alter the legal character of money and so issuing and incorrect W2, or other information return, does not have the power to convert capital into income. When a person receives a W2 from their employer, there are three options:

- Agree with it
- Disagree with it
- Ignore it

Those who ignore an incorrect W2 by refusing to file a return or correct the W2 are in the most danger. If the recipient does not correct it, then it is assumed to be true and the IRS has all the legal authority it needs to collect the tax. The W2 serves as a legal affidavit signed by the employer under penalty of perjury and is assumed to be accurate unless refuted. If unchallenged, it is truth in the eyes of the law.

Those who agree that the money on the W2 is taxable "wages" simply transcribe what is written on the W2 onto their form 1040, sign it under penalty of perjury, and pay the tax. By signing the 1040, the recipient affirms that the money reported on the W2 is taxable income and henceforth is liable for the tax calculated on the form.

Those who disagree with the W2 must formally challenge it. One method is to use the IRS form that was created for taxpayers to correct erroneous W2s: form 4852. This form allows the taxpayer to correct any entries that are believed to be incorrect and then submit it along with the 1040 in lieu of the erroneous W2. This serves as the taxpayer's legal testimony regarding the character of the taxpayer's earnings for the year. The taxpayer signs the 1040 under penalty of perjury, not the employer. People are not doomed to suffer financial injury because an employer issues a W2 in error. So, the form 4852 is a feature of due process giving the injured party the ability to correct and challenge erroneous allegations. If the IRS disagrees with a correction, a contest could begin, but the IRS must prove that capital constitutes "wages as defined." Simple and informed arguments should be decisive: *The money in dispute is capital, and a direct tax on capital must be apportioned.* If the IRS chooses conflict, some battles must be fought.

As shown in section I, "My First Challenge," in 2015 I earned about $140,000 in capital, but only about $29,000 of it was subject to the tax. Most of it qualified as property that may only be taxed via apportionment, but a small portion was taxable as an excise and could be taxed via uniformity; the taxpayer is responsible for recognizing the difference. I had absolutely no "income" in 2015. I corrected the erroneous W2s using the IRS form provided for that purpose, the form 4852, and sent the corrected information to the IRS. The form 1040 and forms 4852 serve as my legal testimony, signed under penalty of perjury, asserting what I believe to be the true and correct character of my earnings and my correctly calculated

CONSTITUTIONAL TAX STRUCTURE

Federal Income Tax liability for the year. The IRS did not challenge those calculations.

The Federal Income Tax does not impose a direct tax on capital, and the IRS knows it. The IRS will return all erroneously withheld property to those Americans who correctly differentiate between their capital and their "income" when calculating their "gross income" on their form 1040; the law requires it. Americans who report their capital as "wages" or as "income" are paying way too much Federal Income Tax.

VIII. Conclusion

The Federal Income Tax is a puzzle and the pieces are scattered between the Constitution, the Internal Revenue Code, Supreme Court rulings, and basic economic concepts. The Internal Revenue Service has been successful in hiding key pieces from the public so that the idea of capital in personal finance has been all but forgotten. In the IRS universe, there is no capital; all money that a person acquires is some form of "income" that can be taxed by the Federal Income Tax. There is no capital in our capitalist society. If employment earnings are income and investment earnings are also income, then how does one acquire capital? Where does capital come from? Does an individual only acquire capital by borrowing from a venture capitalist? Is capital only a business term related to running a business? It only takes a moment of thought to realize that all money cannot be income, and annihilating the idea of individual capital has been a propaganda success for the IRS.

Unfortunately, this is threatening the foundation of our federal system of government. Too many Americans wrongly report their capital as income when they do their federal income taxes. This error causes financial injury to the individual citizen and it sabotages the political and economic sovereignty of the States by allowing the Federal Government to tax capital without apportionment. When

CONSTITUTIONAL TAX STRUCTURE

capital is taxed as income, Americans pay a tax they do not owe and the Internal Revenue Service steals from the State Governments their constitutionally protected source of revenue. Every year, the Federal Government illicitly appropriates revenue that the Constitution has reserved to the States, which forces them into economic dependency requiring "federal funds" to augment their budgets. States are forced to come to Washington, hat in hand, begging for federal money that is nothing more than money taken from their own pockets and returned with federal restrictions. If the IRS was not taxing capital without apportionment, it is likely that the States would never need federal funds and federal aid to States would become a thing of the past.

However, the federal income tax law as written is perfectly constitutional and in legal harmony with every pronouncement of the Supreme Court. It is only through the misapplication of the Internal Revenue Code that capital is being taxed as income. Confusion of terms and economic ignorance allow this misapplication of the law to continue. If Americans woke up tomorrow and began doing their taxes correctly by differentiating between their capital and their income, the whole system would immediately self-correct. Individual financial liberty and the financial balance of power between the State and Federal governments would be instantly restored.

Unfortunately, this system has been operating incorrectly for so long that federal authorities have created a huge mess. So much debt has been created by federal incompetence and mismanagement that if Americans started doing their taxes correctly, and stopped reporting their capital as income, federal revenue would be cut by two thirds overnight. Foreign buyers of US Treasury bonds could lose confidence that the government would ever repay its debt. They would likely stop buying and start selling their Treasury bonds. The value of the dollar could quickly collapse because that value is highly dependent on the sale of Treasury bonds and the pricing of oil in U.S. dollars. The U.S. has lost control over the value of its own currency. If the system self-corrected, we might celebrate the restoration of the Constitution and cheer our financial independence, but it would be a Pyrrhic victory if we woke up to a world where a loaf of bread cost $1,000.

We are living in a time of "passion and delusion," and while it might be hoped that recalling people to the text of the Constitution will quickly correct our problems, a quick solution may not be a wise solution. The Federal Income Tax has been mismanaged for generations by the artful misrepresentation of interested parties in the government. But the interested parties of today did not create this system or the problems that followed. Every citizen, every politician, every bureaucrat, and every judge who is alive today was born into a world where this system was already firmly established. While there are many in positions of power who have embraced the delusion and are actively perpetuating the errors, there are just as many, and maybe more, in government and elsewhere who are just as deceived as the general public. Angry condemnations of government and those who administer it will focus energy on blame instead of solutions. Undermining the credibility of the United States government is in nobody's best interest and will not unwind this problem with any less pain. The problem must be solved. But the solution must be planned, deliberate, and executed in such a manner that it does not destroy the value of our money, our economy, or our country in the process.

The income tax rates ought to be gradually reduced to zero over a period of years, without general knowledge of why this is being done. In addition, legitimate indirect taxes, such as a national sales tax, should be implemented and increased as income tax rates are reduced. However, a national sales tax will never replace the over

CONSTITUTIONAL TAX STRUCTURE

$2 trillion that the Federal Government has been illicitly collecting. The Federal Government must also abandon its extra-constitutional projects and programs. In our federal system of government, the State and the Federal governments have different roles, and there should be minimal duplication of effort between them. James Madison described the roles this way in "Federalist 45":

> The powers reserved to the several States will extend to all the objects which, in the ordinary course of affairs, concern the lives, liberties, and properties of the people, and the internal order, improvement, and prosperity of the State. The operations of the federal government will be most extensive and important in times of war and danger; those of the State governments, in times of peace and security.

The role of the States is to take care of the individual citizens in that State. Taking care of people is not the Federal Government's responsibility. The "lives, liberties, and properties of the people, and the internal order, improvement, and prosperity of the State" is the responsibility of the State Governments. Welfare, education, healthcare, housing, and other issues that affect the lives of individuals living in a State are the responsibility of that State. A State has all revenue derived from direct taxes to address those issues. As was said in Congressional debate:

> But when we come to consider the whole field of taxation, as divided between the two classes of government, I undertake to say that a **very much**

larger sum is raised from the direct form of taxation than from the indirect form.[51]

(emphasis added)

The States would have sufficient financial resources to take care of their own citizens if the IRS wasn't pilfering state treasuries. The Federal Government is stealing the States' revenue and trying to duplicate and do the State Governments' jobs using the States' stolen money. This must end. But the transition will be painful as Social Security, Medicare, student loans, et al. are discarded and the States resume their constitutional duties using their constitutionally protected revenue.

Responsible officials must begin the process of slowly implementing the changes needed to defuse this ticking time bomb. Should the public discover the truth suddenly and before the corrections have been implemented, the credibility of the United States government may never recover.

---

[51] Congressional Record, Vol. L Part IV pg. 3814

Appendices

Appendix A

This is a useful chart that attempts to explain the relationship between capital and income. One can acquire capital from many different sources, and if that capital is invested well, it may produce income. It is the income that is reported on a form 1040, not the capital.

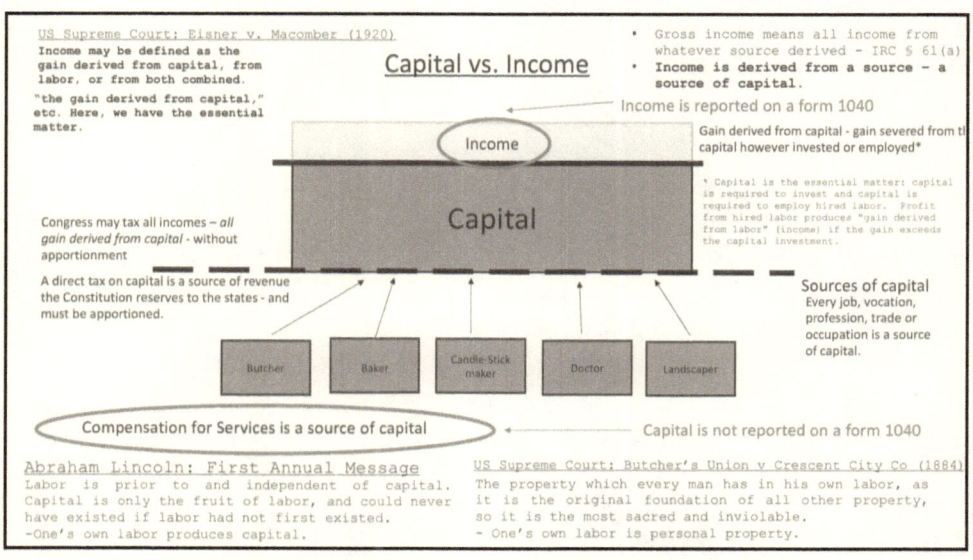

Appendix B

Evolution of "Gross Income"

The 1894 Income Tax did not define "gross income." However, it did contain all of its component parts—"gains or profits" and "income" derived from a "source"—and taxed them differently as described in this book and as explained by *Pollock v. Farmers' Loan and Trust*. The Statues at Large, Vol. 28, Page 553, Chapter 349, Section 27, defines the 1894 tax as:

> SEC. 27. That from and after the first day of January, eighteen hundred and ninety-five, and until the first day of January, nineteen hundred, there shall be assessed, levied, collected, and paid annually upon the **gains, profits, and income** received in the preceding calendar year by every citizen of the United States, whether residing at home or abroad, and every person residing therein, whether said **gains, profits, or income be derived from** any kind of property, rents, interest, dividends, or salaries, or from any profession, trade, employment, or vocation carried on

in the United States or elsewhere, or from any other **source** whatever...

(emphasis added)

The language is clearly recognized as the grandparent of statutory "gross income" found in the 1939 Internal Revenue Title:

> 22(a) GENERAL DEFINITION.—"Gross income" includes gains, profits, and income derived from salaries, wages, or compensation for personal service, of whatever kind and in whatever form paid, or from professions, vocations, trades, businesses, commerce, or sales, or dealings in property, whether real or personal, growing out of the ownership or use of or interest in such property; also from interest, rent dividends, securities, or the transaction of any business carried on for gain or profit, **or gains or profits and income derived from any source whatever**.
>
> **(emphasis added)**

Then as now, "gains or profits" describe capital, while "income" is the "gain derived from capital," or investment gains.

As explained, the 1954 Internal Revenue Code edited the definition of "gross income," ostensibly for simplicity and better organization. This author believes that the revision was purposely crafted to remove the explicit reference to capital described as "gains or profits" from the definition in hopes that modern readers would fail to recognize that both capital and income are being taxed. This confusion would help advance the erroneous idea that all money is income.

What follows is every definition of what the law taxed from 1913 to 1954. In every definition one finds the catchall provision "gains or profits and income derived from any source whatever"—except in the newest 1954 edit. Remember what the Supreme Court said about the importance of that phrase in 1955:

> Such decisions demonstrate that we cannot but ascribe content to the **catchall provision** of § 22(a), "gains or profits and income derived from any source whatever." **The importance of that phrase has been too frequently recognized** since its first appearance in the Revenue Act of 1913 to say now that it adds nothing to the meaning of "gross income."[52]
>
> **(emphasis added)**

REVENUE ACT OF:

1913 38 Stat. 114, 167, ch. 16

> B. That, subject only to such exemptions and deductions as are hereinafter allowed, the net income of a taxable person shall include **gains, profits, and income** derived from salaries, wages, or compensation for personal service of whatever kind and in whatever form paid, or from professions, vocations, businesses, trade, commerce, or sales, or dealings in property, whether real or personal, growing out of the ownership or use of or interest in real or personal property, also from interest, rent, dividends, securities, or the transaction of any lawful business carried on for gain

---

[52] *Commissioner v. Glenshaw Glass Co.*, 348 U.S. 426, 1955

or profit, or *gains or profits and income derived from any source whatever,* including the income from but not the value of property acquired by gift, bequest, devise, or descent:

1916 39 Stat. 756, 757, ch. 463

INCOME DEFINED.

SEC. 2. (a) That, subject only to such exemptions and deductions as are hereinafter allowed, the net income of a taxable person shall include **gains, profits, and income** derived from salaries, wages, or compensation for personal service of whatever kind and in whatever form paid, or from professions, vocations, businesses, trade, commerce, or sales, or dealings in property, whether real or personal, growing out of the ownership or use of or interest in real or personal property, also from interest, rent, dividends, securities, or the transaction of any business carried on for gain or profit, or *gains or profits and income derived from any source whatever:*

1917 40 Stat. 300, 329, ch. 63

SEC. 1200. That subdivision (a) of section two of such Act of September eighth, nineteen hundred and sixteen, is hereby amended to read as follows:

(a) That, subject only to such exemptions and deductions as are hereinafter allowed, the net income of a taxable person shall include **gains, profits, and income**, derived from salaries, wages, or compensation for personal service of whatever kind and in whatever form paid, or from professions, vocations, businesses, trade, commerce, or sales, or dealings in property, whether real or personal, growing out of the ownership or use of or interest in real or personal property, also from interest, rent, dividends, securities, or the transaction of any business carried on for gain or profit, or *gains or profits and income derived from any source whatever.*

1919 40 Stat. 1057, ch. 18

GROSS INCOME DEFINED.

SEC. 213. That for the purposes of this title (except as otherwise provided in section 233) the term "gross income"—

(a) Includes **gains, profits, and income** derived from salaries, wages, or compensation for personal service (including in the case of the President of the United States, the judges of the Supreme and inferior courts of the United States, and all other officers and employees, whether elected or appointed, of the United States, Alaska, Hawaii, or any political subdivision thereof, or the District of Columbia, the compensation received as such), of whatever kind and in whatever form paid, or from professions, vocations, trades, businesses, commerce, or sales, or dealings in property, whether real or personal, growing out of the ownership or use of or interest in such property; also from interest, rent, dividends, securities, or the transaction of any business carried on for gain or profit, or *gains or profits and income derived from any source whatever.*

1921 42 Stat. 227, 237-38, ch. 136

GROSS INCOME DEFINED.

(a) Includes **gains, profits, and income** derived from salaries, wages, or compensation for personal service (including in the case of the President of the United States, the judges of the Supreme and inferior courts of the United States, and all other officers and employees, whether elected or appointed, of the United States, Alaska, Hawaii, or any political subdivision thereof, or the District of Columbia, the compensation received as such), of whatever kind and in whatever form paid, or from professions, vocations, trades, businesses, commerce, or sales, or dealings in property, whether real or personal, growing out of the ownership or use of or interest in such property; also from interest, rent, dividends, securities, or the transaction of any business carried on for gain or profit, or *gains or profits and income derived from any source whatever.*

1924 43 Stat. 253, 267, ch. 234

GROSS INCOME DEFINED.

SEC. 213. For the purposes of this title, except as otherwise provided in section 233—

(a) The term "gross income" includes **gains, profits, and income** derived from salaries, wages, or compensation for personal service (including in the case of the President of the United States, the judges or the Supreme and inferior courts of the United States, and all other officers and employees, whether elected or appointed, of the United States, Alaska, Hawaii, or any political subdivision thereof, or the District of Columbia, the compensation received as such), of whatever kind and in whatever form paid, or from professions, vocations, trades, businesses, commerce, or sales, or dealings in property, whether real or personal, growing out of the ownership or use of or interest in such property; also from interest, rent, dividends, securities, or the transaction of any business carried on for gain or profit, or *gains or profits and income derived from any source whatever.*

1926 44 Stat. 9, 23-24, ch. 27

GROSS INCOME DEFINED

SEC. 213. For the purposes of this title, except as otherwise provided in section 233—

(a) The term "gross income" includes **gains, profits, and income** derived from salaries, wages, or compensation for personal service (including in the case of the President of the United States, the judges of the Supreme and inferior courts of the United States, and all other officers and employees, whether elected or appointed, of the United States, Alaska, Hawaii, or any political subdivision thereof, or the District of Columbia, the compensation received as such), of whatever kind and in whatever form paid, or from professions, vocations, trades, businesses, commerce, or sales, or dealings in property, whether real or personal, growing out of the ownership or use of or interest in such property; also from interest, rent, dividends, securities, or the transaction of any business carried on for gain or profit, or *gains or profits and income derived from any source whatever.*

1928 45 Stat. 791, 797, ch. 852

SEC. 22. GROSS INCOME.

(a) General definition.—"Gross income" includes **gains, profits, and income** derived from salaries, wages, or compensation for personal service, of whatever kind and in whatever form paid, or from professions, vocations, trades, businesses, commerce, or sales, or dealings in property, whether real or personal, growing out of the ownership or use of or interest in such property; also from interest, rent, dividends, securities, or the transaction of any business carried on for gain or profit, or *gains or profits and income derived from any source whatever.*

1932 47 Stat. 169, 178, ch. 209

SEC. 22. GROSS INCOME.

(a) GENERAL DEFINITION.—"Gross income" includes **gains, profits, and income** derived from salaries, wages, or compensation for personal service, of whatever kind and in whatever form paid, or from professions, vocations, trades businesses, commerce, or sales, or dealings in property, whether real or personal, growing out of the ownership or use of or interest in such property; also from interest, rent, dividends, securities, or the transaction of any business carried on for gain or profit, or *gains or profits and income derived from any source whatever.* In the case of Presidents of the United States and judges of courts of the United States taking office after the date of the enactment of this Act, the compensation received as such shall be included in gross income; and all Acts fixing the compensation of such Presidents and judges are hereby amended accordingly.

1934 48 Stat. 680, 686-87, ch. 277

SEC. 22. GROSS INCOME.

(a) GENERAL DEFINITION.—"Gross income" includes **gains, profits, and income** derived from salaries, wages, or compensation for personal service, of whatever kind and in whatever form paid, or from professions, vocations, trades, businesses, commerce, or sales, or dealings in property, whether real or personal, growing out of the ownership or use of or interest in such property; also from interest, rent, dividends, securities, or the transaction of any business carried on for gain or profit, or *gains or profits and income derived from any source whatever.* In the case of Presidents of the United States and judges of courts of the United States taking office after June 6, 1932, the compensation received as such shall be included in gross income; and all Acts fixing the compensation of such Presidents and judges are hereby amended accordingly.

1936 49 Stat. 1648, 1657, ch. 690

SEC. 22. GROSS INCOME.

(a) GENERAL DEFINITION.—"Gross income" includes **gains, profits, and income** derived from salaries, wages, or compensation for personal service, of whatever kind and in whatever form paid, or from professions, vocations, trades, businesses, commerce, or sales, or dealings in property, whether real or personal, growing out of the ownership or use of or interest in such property; also from interest, rent, dividends, securities, or the transaction of any business carried on for gain or profit, or *gains or profits and income derived from any source whatever.* In the case of Presidents of the United States and judges of courts of the United States taking office after June 6, 1932, the compensation received as such shall be included in gross income; and all Acts fixing the compensation of such Presidents and judges are hereby amended accordingly.

1938 52 Stat. 447, 457, ch. 289

SEC. 22. GROSS INCOME.

(a) GENERAL DEFINITION.—"Gross income" includes **gains, profits, and income** derived from salaries, wages, or compensation for personal service, of whatever kind and in whatever form paid, or from professions, vocations, trades, businesses, commerce, or sales, or dealings in property, whether real or personal, growing out of the ownership or use of or interest in such property; also from interest, rent, dividends, securities, or the transaction of any business carried on for gain or profit, or *gains or profits and income derived from any source whatever.* In the case of Presidents of the United States and judges of courts of the United States taking office after June 6, 1932, the compensation received as such shall be included in gross income; and all Acts taxing the compensation of such Presidents and judges are hereby amended accordingly.

1939 53A, Statutes at Large

SEC. 22. GROSS INCOME.

(a) GENERAL DEFINITION.—"Gross income" includes **gains, profits, and income** derived from salaries, wages, or compensation for personal service, of whatever kind and in whatever form paid, or from professions, vocations, trades, businesses, commerce, or sales, or dealings in property, whether real or personal, growing out of the ownership or use of or interest in such property; also from interest, rent, dividends, securities, or the transaction of any business carried on for gain or profit, or *gains or profits and income derived from any source whatever.*

1954 68A, Statues at Large

GENERAL DEFINITION: except as otherwise provided in this subtitle, gross income means all income from whatever source derived, including (but not limited to) the following items:

(1) Compensation for services, including fees, commissions, fringe benefits, and similar items;
(2) Gross income derived from business;
(3) Gains derived from dealings in property;
(4) Interest;
(5) Rents;
(6) Royalties;
(7) Dividends;

(8) Alimony and separate maintenance payments;
(9) Annuities;
(10) Income from life insurance and endowment contracts;
(11) Pensions;
(12) Income from discharge of indebtedness;
(13) Distributive share of partnership gross income;
(14) Income in respect of a decedent; and
(15) Income from an interest in an estate or trust.

For what other purpose does the 1954 definition serve but to edit out "gains or profits"? The purpose of this "simplified" definition is to give the false impression that all money can be taxed as "income."

Appendix C

THE 1913 INCOME TAX

Just a few words will be offered here on the true nature of the 1913 Income Tax and what was intended by its authors.

The purpose of the Income Tax was to reduce the tax burden on the working poor, who had to pay excise taxes on all the goods they purchased while the great accumulations of wealth in the form of investments were relatively untaxed and did not contribute to the support of the Federal Government. The tax was conceived as a *tax the wealth* scheme that levied the tax on one's ability to pay. However, these expressions meant something much different in 1913, as do many financial terms used today.

The 1913 Congressional debates confirm that the Income Tax is a tax-the-wealth scheme designed to relieve those who were taxed when purchasing necessities of life:

> Mr. WILLIAMS. Mr. President, this schedule constitutes to the extent to which it goes the introduction of an entirely new fiscal system. It is, so far as it goes, revolutionary of existing tax methods. The object of levying the tax, of course, is to provide

a revenue, and in addition to that, to a large extent to relieve the backs and the stomachs of people of burdens under the present system and to place those burdens, as far as may be, upon the backs of those who are able to stand them, to begin a system at any rate, of taxing people according to their ability to pay and not according to their necessities.[53]

The phrase "according to their ability to pay" is not used in debate the way we use it today. The tax was, back then as it is today, a tax on the "gain derived from capital"—a tax on investment, not a tax on individual earnings, i.e., the capital itself. Senator Myers noted:

> Fortunately, we will hereafter have an adequate income-tax law by which the accumulators of great wealth, the Morgans and the Rockefellers and men of that class, will pay their just and due proportion of taxes, which they have never done.

The tax was not on the earnings of the average worker, but the wealth accumulated by investment. The income tax imposed a tax on incomes above $4,000, not on earnings above $4,000. In today's dollars, $4,000 is about $90,000. As Senator Lodge said:

> Of course the men of **small *earnings* and small *incomes*** pay taxes to the Government of the United States in the indirect form...

So, one may have earnings from their employment of $4,000 and also an income from their investments of $4,000 (nearly $180,000

---

[53] 1913 Congressional Record, ibid, p. 3772

in today's dollars), and the Income Tax would not even be applied yet. One would only pay the tax when the income exceeded $90,000. This is the concept of taxing according to ability to pay as it was considered in 1913. It is effectively a tax on *walking-around money*— not a tax on money that a family needs to pay bills, buy food, go on vacation, or pay for college. This is what was described by senators in 1913 as an "appropriate standard of living":

> Mr. WILLIAMS. It presumes that where she has the money she ought to pay the tax. The object of it, Mr. President—not to follow up the form of the Senator's question, which would lead me into digressions— was simply this: The House framed its bill upon the theory that **$4,000 was a reasonable amount, in its opinion, for an American family to live upon, with a proper standard of living**, and that a sum below that ought not to be taxed.[54]

In real terms, the exemption has dropped from about $90,000 in 1913 to $20,800[55] today for a married couple. This huge drop results in a much lower standard of living for modern Americans that is then made much worse when one considers that Americans are paying this tax on their capital as well as on their income.

The senators who approved this tax believed that taxing a person according to their ability to pay, by taxing their "incomes" above $4,000, would have very little effect on economic activity. They believed this because the tax, as conceived, did not touch a family's spending money, only the accumulated wealth that was earned in

---

[54] Ibid, p. 3851

[55] 2017 Form 1040 Instructions, p. 8, Chart A.

investments and which thus was money lying around and not being used. Therefore, whether the tax was high or low did not affect the economy. Senator Williams observed:

> The Senator's amendment has a defect that is even greater than that. He forgets that the very beauty, the chief raison d'etre, of an income tax consists in its elasticity. During normal times of peace you have a slight tax upon incomes, graduated not with a view of punishing those who have large incomes, but with a view of equalizing the taxes, because of the greater opportunities that people of large income have to escape taxation than people of small incomes have. In other words, it is equalized in proportion to ability to pay. Then, when the piping times of peace are past and war times come, instead of having to disturb all domestic business by amending the part of the tax law which affects domestic business directly, purposely, or incidentally—one of the three—you merely meet in Congress and raise the income tax one-tenth or one-twentieth or one-fourth or whatever you choose, as to the entire scale or as to some parts of the scale, **leaving the balance untouched.**
>
> One of the virtues of an income tax is that it taxes approximately in accordance with the ability to pay. That is its virtue as far as the payer of the tax is concerned. **Its virtue as far as the Government, the payee, is concerned lies in the elasticity of the**

tax, the ability to raise and lower revenue without disturbing commercial and industrial enterprise.[56]

"Leaving the balance untouched" means only income is taxed, not the capital from which it is derived. This does not describe a tax on earnings or profits. I doubt today's economists or economic thinkers would agree that the modern income tax, as administered, raises revenue without disturbing commercial or industrial enterprise. Yet, that is exactly how it was conceived, and is another example of how the income tax as administered today bears little resemblance to the one enacted in 1913. In legal and constitutional terms, it is no different, but in its administration, the modern income tax inflicts financial injury on the individual and threatens the foundation of our federal system of government because it is applied to capital as well as income.

---

[56] 1913 Congressional Record, p. 3806

Appendix D

CLARIFYING TERMS

In an effort to obscure the idea of capital in personal finance, the IRS has attached every imaginable adjective to "income" in an attempt to obliterate the distinction between income and principal. According to the IRS, all money a person receives is some kind of "income," as if capital does not exist.

The key to understanding these terms is to remember that all income is derived from capital, and income will always retain the character of the capital from which it is derived. An adjective modifying "income" distinguishes one type of "gain derived from capital" from another.

- Earned Income: Income derived from earned capital. If a person earns capital through their own effort and then invests some of that earned capital, the gain derived from earned capital is earned income.
- Unearned Income: Income derived from unearned capital. This usually occurs when a person inherits investments or real estate that produces income. The recipient did not earn

the capital that is producing the income and thus gain derived from unearned capital is unearned income.
- <u>Business Income</u>: Income derived from business capital. If a business invests some of its surplus capital and it produces a gain, the gain derived from business capital is business income. The invested capital belongs to the business and so does the income derived from it.
- <u>Individual Income</u>: Income derived from individual capital. Gain derived from an individual's capital is individual income. It can be earned or unearned.
- <u>Ordinary Income</u>: Individual or business income.
- <u>Wage Income</u>: Ridiculous oxymoron. Wages from privileged activity are taxed as an excise and included in the "gross income" calculation, but the wages themselves are capital.

Appendix E

Taxing Privilege

Some readers may be unfamiliar with the idea of taxing privilege. In short, taxing privilege—a well-established feature of American law—is a legal ruse that permits the Federal Government to tax property without going through the rule of apportionment. The government can then argue that the privilege is being taxed, not the property itself. The difference between taxing property and privilege is described by the Supreme Court in *Knowlton v. Moore* (1900):

> They are based on two principles: 1. An inheritance tax is not one on property, but one on the succession. 2. The right to take property by devise or descent is the creature of the law, and not a natural right—a privilege, and therefore the authority which confers it may impose conditions upon it.

So, financial gains that are a "creature of the law," like inheritance and alimony, etc., are acquired by privilege, which may be taxed as an excise. In practical application, the tax is based on the amount of property, but legally it is the privilege being taxed—not the property being transferred.

There are many who believe that the defining feature of the Federal Income Tax is privilege. It has been argued that in order for money to qualify for the tax, it must be acquired by some kind of privilege that brings it within the authority of the Federal Government to tax it as an excise. Otherwise, money is property that must be taxed by apportionment. While this work has referred to privilege as an element of the tax, it hasn't focused on it as the defining element of the tax. Instead, it has focused on the distinction between income and principal and emphasized that "income" cannot be money that is capital or property. Also, it has stated that "gross income" includes both an indirect tax on income and an indirect tax on capital. However, an excise tax on privilege is an indirect tax on capital.

For those who would like to focus on the privilege element of the tax, it can be explained by recalling the Supreme Court's pronouncement in *Doyle v. Mitchell Bros Co.* (1918):

> Whatever difficulty there may be about a precise and scientific definition of "income," it imports, as used here, something entirely distinct from principal or capital either as a ***subject of taxation*** or as a ***measure of the tax.***
>
> **(emphasis added)**

Both income and principal may be either the subject of a tax or the measure of the tax. So, an object that may be untaxable if it is the subject of a tax may still be used as the measure of the tax, as described in *Stratton's Independence Ltd. V. Howbert* (1913):

> Congress, in exercising the right to tax a legitimate subject of taxation as a franchise or privilege, was not debarred by the Constitution from measuring the taxation by the total income, although derived in part from property which, considered by itself, was not taxable.

This principle is further described by F. Morse Hubbard:

> The income tax is, therefore, not a tax on income as such. It is an excise tax with respect to certain activities and privileges which is measured by reference to the income which they produce. **The income is not the subject of the tax: it is the basis for determining the amount of tax.**[57]
>
> **(emphasis added)**

So, regarding the tax on "income," the subject of the tax is the *privilege* of carrying any activity or owing any property that produces income. The income is the *measure of the tax*; the more income one earns from investments, the more tax one pays for the privilege.

Considering "gains or profits," the subject of the tax is the *privilege* of acquiring capital from federally connected employment, from a creature of the law (i.e., without working for it), or from doing business in corporate form. The capital is the *measure of the tax*; the more capital one earns, the more tax one pays for the privilege. If capital is the subject of the tax, then it is a tax on property and thus a direct tax (within the meaning of the Constitution) that must be apportioned.

---

[57] 1943 Congressional Record, 78th Congress Volume 89 Part 2, pg. 2580

So, essentially the tax can be explained as a tax on privilege. But even when analyzing the tax from this perspective, the distinction between the income and the principal must be maintained: when taxing privilege, either income or principal may be used as the measure of the tax, and they must be separate and distinct from each other.

www.ingramcontent.com/pod-product-compliance
Lightning Source LLC
Chambersburg PA
CBHW020426220526
45464CB00002B/587